Penguin Books
Proust's Last Beer

Bob Arnebeck is an avid reader of the obituaries and has a B.A. in literature. Allen Appel is an avid reader of Victorian magazines, with scissors always handy, and he has a B.A. in psychology. Not a few of their collaborative efforts have appeared in the *Washington Post Sunday Magazine*.

Proust's Last Beer

A History of Curious Demises

by Bob Arnebeck
Art by Allen Appel

Penguin Books

To Marion

Penguin Books Ltd, Harmondsworth,
Middlesex, England
Penguin Books, 625 Madison Avenue,
New York, New York 10022, U.S.A.
Penguin Books Australia Ltd, Ringwood,
Victoria. Australia
Penguin Books Canada Limited, 2801 John Street,
Markham, Ontario, Canada L3R 1B4
Penguin Books (N.Z.) Ltd, 182-190 Wairau Road,
Auckland 10, New Zealand

First published 1980

LIBRARY OF CONGRESS CATALOGING IN PUBLICATION DATA
Arnebeck, Bob.
  Proust's last beer.
  1. Death — Anecdotes, facetiae, satire, etc.
2. Last words. I. Title.
PN6268. D35A7   080   80-16104
ISBN 0 14 00.5022 1

Printed in the United States of America by
Capital City Press, Inc., Montpelier, Vermont
Set in ITC Meridien 54

Some of the art by Allen Appel is based on material taken from the following titles in the Dover Pictorial Archive Series published by Dover Publications, Inc., to whom grateful acknowledgment is made: *293 Renaissance Woodcuts for Artists and Illustrators: Jost Amman's Kunstbuchlein* by Jost Amman; *Victorian Fashions and Costumes*, edited by Stella Blum; *Curious Woodcuts of Fanciful and Real Beasts* by Konrad Gesner; *Handbook of Plant and Floral Ornament* by Richard G. Hatton; and especially *Devils, Demons, Death and Damnation* by Ernst and Johanna Lehner.

"Railroad Bill" from *American Murder Ballads,* compiled by Olive W. Burt, reprinted by permission of Olive W. Burt

Contents

1

Death à la Carte

Two Hours after eating

a dozen oysters washed down with Evian mineral water
leg of lamb
fried potatoes
beans washed down with a bottle of ginger soda
monte bianco for dessert with two bottles of Coca-Cola and two oranges

King Farouk smoked a Havana Cigar and died.

Harry Jellinek, a fifty-year-old auto mechanic, bought two seed rolls at the Horn & Hardart Cafeteria at Broadway and 104th Street. He sprinkled cyanide on both rolls, ate part of one, felt sick, staggered to the men's room, and died.

Lillian Rosenfield, a forty-three-year-old scavenger, saw the seed rolls. She stashed the uneaten one into her bag and gobbled down the half-eaten roll. She died before she got out of the Horn & Hardart door. (After searching Rosenfield's basement apartment, police found a key to a safety deposit box. She had five savings accounts that totaled over $41,000.).

A jury in Pennsylvania sentenced Joshua Jones to be hanged for the murder of his wife. In his last days Jones craved more than his prison fare. He sold rights to his body to a doctor for ten dollars. With that money Jones treated himself to delicacies. When execution day arrived, he still had one dollar left. He put it between two pieces of bread and ate it.

8
Proust's
Last Beer

Delicacies for the Dying

As the consumptive Elizabeth Barrett Browning suffered through her final hours, her poet-husband spoon-fed her fowl jelly.

Poet Alexander Pushkin's wife fed her fatally wounded husband blackberries in syrup.

Robert Louis Stevenson expired while making his special mayonnaise for his wife's salad.

The state hung Elizabeth Van Valkenburgh for trying to cure her husband of his drinking problem, even though the cure — arsenic in his tea — was very successful.

At 2:00 A.M. Dylan Thomas climbed out of bed and said he was thirsty. He went out. At 3:30 A.M. he came back to bed, boasting to his wife before he went to sleep, "I've had eighteen straight whiskies. I think that's the record."

He died five days later.

As the French encyclopedist Denis Diderot reached for an apricot at dinner, his wife told him not to eat it.

"How in the devil can it hurt me?" he snapped at his wife.

He ate the apricot, and as he reached for some stewed cherries, he coughed slightly and slumped down on the table, dead.

One morning Lord Castlereagh, the British foreign minister, scolded his maid "for some fault in his breakfast." That fault, according to the painter and journalist Benjamin Hayden, was "hot buttered toast," which Castlereagh's doctor forbade him to eat. For good reason. Hayden explains what happened after temptation overtook his lordship and he ate the forbidden toast: "His brain filled with more blood, and he became insane!" He rushed to his room and slit his throat with a pen knife.

The pirate Bartholomew Roberts was eating red-hot West Indian pickles called salamagundi for breakfast when his crew warned him of the approach of a British warship. Roberts couldn't tear himself away from the spicy delight. Only when the warship was about to attack did Roberts push himself away from his breakfast and rush onto the deck.

The first shot from the warship struck Roberts in the throat, killing the aftertaste of red-hot salamagundi, and Roberts.

Morris Slater, a.k.a. Railroad Bill, looted freight cars in Alabama and Florida. He also killed a sheriff, a deputy, and a detective. So when a posse sneaked up on Slater in a grocery store in Atmore, Alabama, they didn't ask him to surrender:

> Railroad Bill eatin' crackers an' cheese,
> Long came a sheriff, chipper as you please,
> Was lookin' for Railroad Bill.

> Railroad Bill lyin' on the grocery floor,
> Got shot two times an' two times more.
> No more lookin' for Railroad Bill.

12
Proust's
Last Beer

President Franklin Roosevelt died at his vacation retreat in Warm Springs, Georgia. Today, visitors can see there an unfinished portrait of Roosevelt. While it was being painted, FDR groaned, "I have a terrible headache," rubbed his temples, and collapsed. Ironically, earlier that day Roosevelt had taken his draft card out and torn it up, saying that he wouldn't need it anymore. No one knows what became of FDR's torn draft card. But the shopping list he wrote out that morning —

    24 oranges
     4 hog feet
     5 turnip greens
    12 lemons
    12 grapefruit
     1 lb. ground round
     1 lb. beef stew
     2 lettuce
     2 celery
     1 asparagus

— is framed on the wall of the museum at Warm Springs.

Succumbing to pneumonia, Marcel Proust retouched some of the literary portraits he painted in his novel *Remembrance of Things Past*. "Now that I'm in the same condition myself, I want to add some notes to the death of Bergotte," he told his maid and asked her to take dictation.

"'But I couldn't have champagne, for instance?'
'Why certainly, if you feel like it.'

> Unable to believe our ears, we send for the very brands
> we had most strictly denied ourselves; and it is such
> things as this that impart a certain slight vulgarity
> to the unbelievable frivolousness of the dying —"

But that is fiction. In the morning, before he died, Proust sent to the Ritz, not for champagne but for iced beer.

Russian playwright Anton Chekhov did have champagne, on his doctor's orders.

"I haven't had champagne for ages," Chekhov said.

He drained his glass, rolled over on his left side, and died.

Beethoven's doctor prescribed champagne and good German wine to ease his patient's dropsy. But Vienna had no German wine fine enough to satisfy the maestro's palate; he drank Krumpholz-Kirchener and Grinzinger wines while he waited for a shipment of choice wine from Mainz. A case of Rudesheimer Berg 1806 finally arrived too late for any of it to touch the dying Beethoven's lips. However, it did earn his last words: "Pity, pity, too late."

As a rare March storm rolled over the Vienna hills, a blaze of lightning and a clap of thunder reached a glowing crescendo. The great composer opened his eyes, raised a clenched fist, and died.

As Mary Wollstonecraft was dying of childbed fever, her doctor put puppies on her nipples to relieve the milk. She took the treatment cheerfully, and when the doctor added frequent and ample doses of red wine to the regimen, his patient became almost blissful. "Oh Godwin," she cried out to her husband, the noted philosopher William Godwin, "I am in Heaven!"

But Godwin would not allow such maudlin religious sentiments to mar the death of one of England's great radicals. He rephrased her cry: "You mean, my dear, that your symptoms are a little easier."

At a party in Bucharest, Lieutenant Jon Jonescu offered a young woman a glass of beer, warning her that if she didn't drink the beer he'd shoot himself. She laughed and refused the drink.

He shot himself.

As the Navy cutter *Pearl* chased Blackbeard's pirate ship off the North Carolina coast, the pirate grabbed a glass of liquor and drank a fierce toast to the captain of the *Pearl*. "Damnation seize my soul if I give you any quarter or take any from you!"

It was the pirate's last drink. Twenty-five wounds later, Blackbeard's head was on a pike on the *Pearl*'s bowsprit.

First Prince Yussupov tried using poisoned cakes to kill Rasputin, the monk who seemed to have bewitched the Romanov rulers of Russia. But Rasputin ate them all and asked for more. Yussupov poured him poisoned wine. Rasputin gulped it down with no ill effects. Out of patience, Yussupov shot Rasputin. A doctor declared Rasputin dead. But as Yussupov walked away from the corpse, he felt a hand on his shoulder; Rasputin ran past his assassins and out into the courtyard. Finally Yussupov and his friends clubbed the monk to death. They loaded him into a car and threw him off the Petrovsky Bridge.

But that's Yussupov's version. Rasputin's daughter Maria doubts it. "I'm positive," she wrote, "that my father did not eat the poisoned cakes, for he had a horror of sweet things."

Doctors in the Victorian era ascribed many of the deaths that came after eating to a disease called "cholera morbus." When two sisters, Mrs. Elizabeth Dunning and Mrs. Joshua Deane, died after eating corn fritters, their doctor suspected cholera morbus. But the coroner probed deeper and found another culprit. The sisters had also just eaten a sweet gift from Mr. Dunning's secret mistress; very sweet — homemade bonbons laced with arsenic.

Early on Sunday, July 4, President Zachary Taylor began munching green apples. But after officiating at the laying of the cornerstone for the Washington Monument, "Old Rough and Ready" naturally switched to cherries. His doctor warned him to slow down on the roughage, but the president munched cherries well into the night.

The next morning the president had stomach pains and fever. Four days later "Old Rough and Ready" was dead.

DEATH OF JULIAN THE APOSTATE.

Health faddist Sylvester Graham developed a vitamin-filled brown flour and called it graham flour. But when Graham himself was very sick he rejected his graham crackers and milk in favor of a dose of Congress water and a tepid bath. He died soon after.

MacDonald Clark, the "Mad Poet of Broadway," was often in his cups, but he didn't die of the hard stuff. He drowned himself in a sink.

The gangster Arthur Flegenheimer, aka Dutch Schultz, was gunned down by the Mob while he dined at the Palace Chophouse. He lingered long enough to make a statement full of delirious ravings about his mother and his life of crime to the police. But at the end, Dutch remembered a final obligation: "Please help me up, Henry. Max, come over here. French Canadian bean soup. I want to pay. Let them leave me alone."

The gangster had his faults, but he wasn't one to run out on a check.

Beyond Baedeker's

Bishop James Pike, the popular American religious leader, and his wife, Diana, honeymooned in Israel. They rented a Ford Cortina at the Tel Aviv airport and, equipped with two Coca-Colas and a road map provided by Avis, drove toward Qumran, the site where the Dead Sea scrolls were found.

The temperature climbed to 130° F. The rough road seemed to lead into endless desert. The bishop put his faith in the map and told his wife to drive on. The right rear wheel of the Ford got stuck in a rut. They drank their last Coke and started walking. The scene reminded Diana of the movie *Lawrence of Arabia.* She took pictures.

Later, dying of thirst, Bishop Pike urinated on his fingers and moistened her lips. He washed his mouth out with urine and she drank some. "Then," she wrote later, "he let his urine flow and we both took it and washed it all over our faces and arms."

They walked until he could go no further. She resolved to stay and die with him. He told her to go on.

"If I die here," he told her, "I am at peace, and I have no regrets."

She made it to a work camp. Rescuers found his body six days later, far from the road to Qumran, in the Wadi Mashash.

In 1926 Colonel Fawcett, the famous British explorer, went to the jungles of South America to find the stone tower that glowed with what the Indians called "the light that never goes out." Beyond that he expected to find the falls that sink into the earth where Indian legend said "in the quiet water the figure of a man carved in white rock moves to and from with the force of the current." And beyond that Fawcett knew he'd find "the lost city of Z."

Deep in the bush at Dead Horse Camp, Mato Grosso, Brazil, Fawcett wrote to his wife in England, "you need have no fear of failure."

No further letter — nor Fawcett — ever came out of the area the Indians also called "the land of no return."

22
Proust's
Last Beer

In 1913 Ambrose Bierce, journalist and author of *The Devil's Dictionary,* wrote:

> Goodbye, if you hear of my being stood up against a Mexican stone wall and shot to rags please know that I think it is a pretty good way to depart this life. It beats old age, disease, or falling down the cellar stairs. To be a Gringo in Mexico —ah, that's euthanasia!

The seventy-two-year-old writer went to help the Mexican rebel Pancho Villa and was never heard from again.

A valet at the Ritz Hotel in Paris found movie star Olive Thomas lying naked on a sable opera cape. Her Parisian shopping spree had gotten out of hand, winding up with a wild night at the Dead Rat in Montmartre, an orgy of champagne and cocaine, and finally, a drug-induced coma.

Doctors rushed her to the American Hospital where before she died she explained, "Well, Doc, this is what Paris did for me."

During World War I the writers and twin sisters Gladys Louise and Dorothea Crowell volunteered to be nurses in France. Both had rough times. In a poem, "The Deep," Gladys wrote:

> I must have peace, increasing peace, such as the ocean keeps.

When peace came, they boarded a ship for America. But the horizon wasn't peaceful enough. After the ship left harbor, they both jumped.

At 3:00 A.M., Leo Tolstoy awoke to the sound of his personal papers being shuffled: Sonya, his wife of forty-three years, was spying on him again. The eighty-two-year-old novelist checked his pulse. It was ninety-seven, too high, so he decided to clear out. He left a letter behind instructing Sonya not to try to track him down.

Russia's greatest writer headed for the Caucasus but had difficulty traveling incognito, since even illiterate peasants recognized the bearded patriarch. Newspapers splashed his flight on their front pages. To escape all the attention, he sat alone on the train's observation platform but caught a bad cold there. His doctor ordered him off the train at Astapova and installed him in the stationmaster's quarters.

Journalists, photographers, and secret police aboard a special train hired by Sonya hurried to the little town. For days Tolstoy's every utterance on love, charity, etcetera, as well as the final entries in his secret diary, were reported around the world. Once he cried out, "Ah, what a bother . . ."

Only when he lost consciousness did the doctors let Sonya rush to his side; she kissed him and begged, "Forgive me, forgive." He died.

En route to the Council of Lyons, Thomas Aquinas became lost in thought. His donkey, left to its own devices, plodded on under a low-hanging limb. The theologian struck his head and died soon after. The world grieved, but not as much as the donkey. Legend claims that when it saw the saint's bier, it dropped dead.

In his book *The History of Sandford and Merton,* Thomas Day taught children that animals served man best when treated with kindness. The writer practiced what he preached, riding unbroken colts and taming them with his gentle restraint. Only one wild colt reacted in a manner suggesting that there were dangers in the

26
Proust's
Last Beer

philosophy Day espoused; the skittish young horse threw Day as he journeyed to his mother's. But the author was in no shape for a revised edition. He died of a concussion an hour later.

D. H. Lawrence, dying of tuberculosis, was in no shape to travel. But as he lay in bed on his last day, he asked his wife to read him *The Life of Columbus.* Was Lawrence preparing for a new world? In his last delirium he asked his wife to hold his ankle.

> O let my ankles be bathed in moonlight, that I may go
> sure and moon-shod, cool and bright-footed
> towards my goal.

A morphine injection calmed him. He told her, "I am better now; if I could only sweat I would be better." He fell asleep. Then there were gaps in his breathing, his cheeks and jaw sank, and he died.

The British explorer Captain James Cook wanted to teach some thieving natives a lesson. With a handful of marines, he went ashore to take a Hawaiian chief as hostage until the natives behaved. Even though he was greeted by a mob armed with stones and daggers, Cook remained calm; he and his crew had guns. A native tried to stab one of Cook's men. Cook fired at him but a war shield deflected the bullet. The natives attacked. "Take to the boats," Cook shouted to his men. His retreat was cut short; the natives captured, stabbed, and drowned him.

Later they returned his remains. The lot — scalp, bones picked clean, and both hands preserved in salt—weighed a little more than nine pounds. After due honors, all nine pounds were buried at sea.

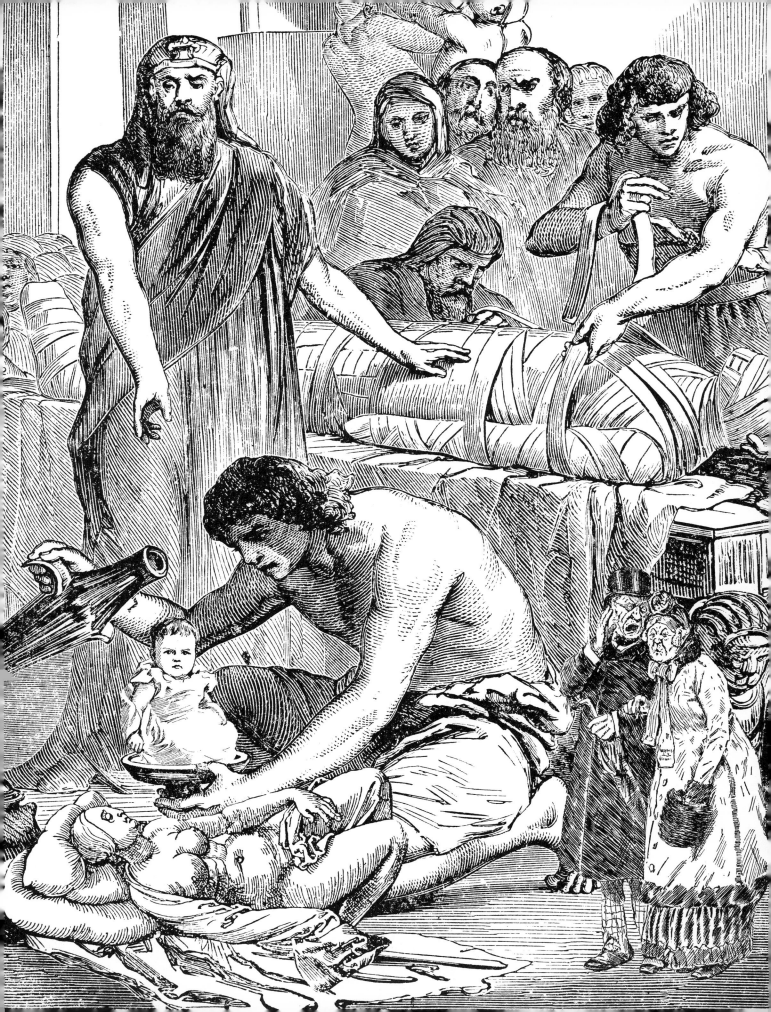

William Pitt was touring an art gallery in Bath, England, when he heard galloping.

"That must be a courier with news for me," said the British statesman. He opened the packet. "Heavy news indeed." Napoleon had won at Austerlitz.

Sickened, Pitt went home to Putney. When he entered his mansion he saw a map of Europe on the wall.

"Roll up that map," he ordered.

Delirious his last night, he raved about a mission he had sent to Berlin in a final effort to check Napoleon. He kept asking the direction of the wind.

"East, that will do, that will bring him quick."

Just before the end he cried: "Oh, my country! How I leave my country!"

In 1788 Henry Beaufoy of the Association for Promoting the Discovery of the Interior Parts of Africa spread a map before the American explorer John Ledyard and traced a line from Cairo to Sennar, and then into unknown West Africa. Ledyard, Beaufoy wrote, "said he should think himself singularly fortunate to be entrusted with the Adventure. I asked him when he would set out. 'Tomorrow morning,' was his answer."

But the source of the Niger was not to be found by such an impatient man. The British consul in Cairo wrote to Beaufoy:

> A day was fixed for set off, but bad weather or other causes occasioned delay as happens to most caravans. Mr. Ledyard took offence at the delay and threw himself into a violent rage . . . which deranged something in his system that he thought to cure by an emetic. . . . Excessive vomiting ensued, in consequence of which he broke a blood vessel and died.

30
Proust's
Last Beer

Aldous Huxley lay dying of throat cancer in Santa Barbara, California. Around noon he scribbled on his writing pad: "LSD — Try It/intramuscular/100 mm." His wife asked the doctor if she could administer the drug. The doctor gave his consent. Huxley's last trip ended at 5:20 P.M., November 22, 1963.

DEATH OF WAT TYLER

3
Skills That Killed

While riding through the snow in the early spring, Sir Francis Bacon wondered if cold delayed putrefaction of tissue. When his carriage passed a farmyard he saw an opportunity for experimentation. He bought a chicken, had it killed, and promptly stuffed it with snow. Thus, Bacon learned that cold does delay putrefaction. He also got bronchitis and died less than a fortnight after the chicken.

His skill in curing mad people made Reverend John Ashbourne's house in Suffolk, England, the earliest psychiatric clinic. The clinic closed in 1661 when a patient ran Rev. Ashbourne through with a pitchfork.

While surveying the site for the Brooklyn Bridge, chief engineer John Roebling stood on a cluster of piles at the Fulton Ferry slip taking signals from an assistant. Roebling didn't notice a ferry enter the slip. The ferry crashed into the rack fender. The rack fender lurched toward the piles, catching Roebling's foot.

After amputation of his toes, lockjaw set in. But the engineer kept working. On the day before he died he designed a machine to help lift and move him from his bed.

As he lugged his easels, canvas, and paints back to his house to escape a storm, Cézanne collapsed. A laundry-cart driver found the old man and took him home. The next day Cézanne went out again but was too weak to paint. Confined

34
Proust's
Last Beer

to his house, he didn't idle. He wrote a letter to his paint supplier: "It is now over a week since I asked you to send me ten Burnt Lakes 7, and I have had no reply. What's going on? Please reply promptly."

Even in his last delirium Cézanne's mind was on his work.

"Pontier! Pontier!" He yelled the name of the museum director who refused to show his work, and died.

Antoine Blisonnette, a thirty-five-year-old factory worker in Montreal, yawned on the job. Then she couldn't shut her jaws. After an operation at the hospital to close her mouth, she died.

As he ended Don Carlo's aria *"Urne fatale del mio destino"* in Verdi's opera *La Forza del Destino,* baritone Leonard Warren spread his arms out in triumph, received a loud ovation, and fell flat on his face. Some in the audience laughed.

Tenor Richard Tucker rushed onstage crying, "Lenny! Lenny!" Stagehands carried the stricken baritone backstage. Metropolitan Opera director Rudolf Bing quickly telephoned another baritone who could finish the opera. The audience waited restlessly for twenty-five minutes. Then Bing parted the gold curtain and faced the audience.

"This," Bing began, "is one of the saddest nights in the history of the Metropolitan" —(gasps of "no!" from the audience)—"may I ask you all to rise"—(some began to sob)—"in memory of one of our greatest performers who died in the midst of one of his greatest performances."

Pliny's daughter saw the unusual cloud first. She called to her father. The author of a thirty-seven-volume natural history wanted a closer look. He ordered a ship to take him to Vesuvius.

While others fled, Pliny took a house close to the volcano. He dictated his observations, took a bath, had supper. When the house started shaking, he decided that it wasn't safe to stay under a roof. Flanked by his aides and with a pillow tied to his head, he tried to dodge the pumice peppering the fields. They reached the sea, but the waves kept their boat in. The heat was unbearable, especially for the portly natural philosopher. To cool himself he lay prostrate next to a stream, but the killing fumes came closer. He had to move. He tried to lift himself, then tried again. He fell back down dead, a victim of the eruption that buried Pompeii.

Dr. Joseph Price was in a hospital suffering from a retroperitoneal infection. But down the hall there was a difficult appendectomy to be done. The renowned abdominal surgeon (Price was the man who separated gynecology from abdominal surgery) left his bed to do the job.

The next day Price suffered violent pains. He recognized the symptoms and told his fellow surgeons how to operate. They did their best, but it wasn't enough. And soon there was no Dr. Price to tell them what to do next.

In the afternoon Dr. Daniel Brainard lectured a class on the local cholera situation. That evening he began writing an article on cholera. The next morning he had cholera. That night, he died.

38
Proust's
Last Beer

During her medical studies in Paris antivivisectionist Anna Kingsford approached Dr. Claude Bernard, a world-famous researcher, invoked the wrath of God upon him, and collapsed at his feet. Bernard died a few days later. Kingsford credited herself with his death and went after an even more famous medical researcher, Louis Pasteur. Again and again she invoked the wrath of God upon Pasteur. She made frequent attacks on his laboratory. After one of her forays Pasteur did get sick. But so did she. Pasteur recovered, but she did not. In fact, Pasteur survived her by seven years.

Even after catching a bad cold, Mary Baker Eddy sat at her desk issuing commands that kept her Church of Christian Science going. She believed that no disease, let alone a cold, could kill her. Only Malicious Animal Magnetism could kill her by "mental murder."

When her cold became worse, she summoned followers to surround her and battle the evil force aimed at her by enemies. She fought until the last, open-eyed and silent, without the least acknowledgment of death.

Messrs. Burke and Hare weren't getting rich running a seedy inn in Edinburgh. One night an old lodger died. Deciding to make some extra income, Burke and Hare sold the body to the medical school. Eager for more easy money, and too impatient to wait on nature, they began smothering their lodgers while they slept. They could soon afford to live high. One night they were enjoying the company of a beautiful Edinburgh whore when Burke's wife barged in. Quickly, Burke demonstrated that this meeting was only business — his business. He smothered the whore and carted her off to the medical school.

Rather than dissect the corpse, doctors pickled it in whiskey and used it in muscle control and development classes. Not only medical students flocked to see the beauty — artists did too. So did the police.

Hare told on Burke. Burke was hanged. The medical school passed up his corpse.

The great actor Edwin Booth was dying. A crowd of reporters and admirers waited outside his room. A little after 1:00 A.M. a thunderstorm struck. All the lights in the house went out. A voice cried out, "Don't let Father die in the dark!"

The lights came up, and the great actor died.

They found the sixty-eight-year-old sportswriter at the *San Francisco Morning Telegraph* peacefully slumped over his desk. They nudged him, but Bat Masterson, the hero of Dodge City, was dead.

I dreamed I was back in battle. I waded in blood up to my knees. I saw death as it is on the battle field. The poor boys with arms shot off and legs gone were lying on the ground. . . . Once again I stood by them and witnessed those soldiers bearing their soldier pains, limbs being sawed off without opiates being taken or even a bed to lie on. I crept around once more, trying to give them at least a drink of water . . . and I heard them at last speak of mothers and wives and sweethearts, but never a murmur of complaint. Then I awoke to hear myself groan because I have a stupid pain in my back. . . .

Two days later nurse Clara Barton succumbed to double pneumonia, crying out at the end, "Let me go! Let me go!" It was only an echo of faraway battlefields. She died peacefully in her bed in Glen Echo, Maryland.

42
Proust's
Last Beer

Senator Stephen A. Douglas was dying in Chicago, but his delirious mind was still in the Senate. While a doctor tended to his fever, Douglas cried out, "Stop, there are twenty against me, the measure is defeated!" Death cast the deciding vote.

Dr. Pinchbeck hired John Coan to entertain at his tavern. Coan was only three feet tall, and when he stood on tables and sang songs, Pinchbeck made many pennies. Alas, wee John died of overwork. Pinchbeck hated to let go of his gimmick, so he hung John Coan's effigy over his tavern door, and jolly men flocked to drink under the sign of the Little Dead Man.

The famous clown, James Clement Boswell, created the broken ladder trick. As he climbed a ladder he pulled each rung out and threw it away. At the top of the ladder, he pushed away one stile and stood on his head on the other. The feat was entertaining but deleterious to the performer. While doing it in 1859, Boswell had a stroke. He came down the ladder the hard way and died soon after.

A butcher in Barcelona heard from a friend that his wife was seeing another man. He hurried home and found her alone. To celebrate her fidelity he took her out to a show, but she was unusually quiet all night.

The next morning the butcher went to his refrigerator to take out the meat for market. As he swung open the door, the body of his rival fell out. He didn't have much to say either.

4
The Sporting Death

When not entertaining pretty young women in the special room of his sham Tudor house called "The Flirtorium," playwright W. S. Gilbert (of Gilbert and Sullivan) liked to invite them out for sport, a swim in his private lake. One hot May day the seventy-four-year-old Gilbert invited Miss Ruby Preece and Miss Winifred Emery out for a swim. The girls went in first, and in moments Miss Preece was out of her depth.

"It's not very deep, don't splash. You'll be all right!" Gilbert gave one cheer more before he dove in for the rescue. When he reached her he commanded, "Put your hands on my shoulders, and don't struggle."

She obeyed. He suffered a heart attack and sank. She went under, too, but her toes found the mud and she made it to shore. Gilbert did not.

All six feet six inches and 280 pounds of defensive tackle Big Daddy Lipscomb was dead. Police said he died of an overdose of heroin. His teammates on the Pittsburgh Steelers said that couldn't be true. Big Daddy was afraid of needles.

The seventeenth-century philosopher Michel de Montaigne admired quick, uncomplicated deaths. "The deadest deaths are best," was how he put it. In one of his essays he cites his brother's swift quietus after a game of tennis as a perfect example. His brother, writes Montaigne, "received a blow with a ball that hit him a little above the right ear, without the appearance of any contusion, bruise or hurt." He died only six hours later. The philosopher made no comment on the dangers of tennis. He didn't even note if his brother had been playing the net.

Baseball star Michael J. Kelly performed in vaudeville during the off-season, singing and boasting of his feats on the diamond. In November 1894 he left New York by boat to fill an engagement at the Palace in Boston. He caught pneumonia. When he reached Boston, friends rushed him to the hospital. As they slipped him off the stretcher, Kelly murmured, "This is my last slide."

The morning papers gave the baseball great his last headline: "At 9:55 last night 'King Kelly' heard the decision of the Great Umpire from which there is no appeal. ..."

Perhaps the cruelest chess player of them all, Ivan the Terrible fed bishops to the bears. He had his master of the horse stripped, hung by the heels, and minced by four swordsmen. He sacrificed human pawns by the thousands, feeding them to huge pike and carp. He sent his queen to a nunnery.

Then Ivan began "grievously to swell in the cods." He tried all sorts of cures for this male complaint but got relief only from soaking in the tub for hours. After one bath he summoned his nobles and challenged one to a game of chess. As he placed the king on the board, Ivan collapsed, "strangled and stark dead."

Death Dive

The death-defying birdman Lincoln Beachey powered his sleek monoplane over a crowd of fifty thousand at the Panama-Pacific Exposition in San Francisco. He looped-the-loop as he climbed to five thousand feet, then pointed his monoplane straight down for his famous "Death Dive." Usually Beachey's skills told him just when to pull out, but he had never flown over two hundred miles an hour before. When he tugged at his controls, both wings snapped in two, and he plunged into San Francisco Bay. The birdman's dangerous stunt finally lived up to its name.

48
Proust's
Last Beer

Robert Overbeck survived the Bataan Death March (the death toll was 1800) and was one of the five men rescued from a torpedoed Japanese prison ship. Death caught up to Overbeck in Costa Rica where he quietly collapsed after a game of tennis in 1972.

Cuba tied Haiti with only nine minutes left in their crucial soccer match. A member of Haiti's elite palace guard banged his rifle down in anger. The rifle fired. The bullet killed the guard instantly. More shots rang out in the packed stadium Eight people were killed. And the battle on the field ended in a tie.

Before going fishing, Mrs. Margaret Patzsch went out in her backyard to catch some live bait. It should have been easy with her new electric worm catcher. *Pace* Mrs. Patzsch: electrocuted.

While sculptor Henry Hering was teeing off at his country club in Scarsdale, a B-25 bomber crashed into the north side of the Empire State Building, killing ten people. The outer wall of the building sheared off the plane's wing. The fuselage and engines ripped an eighteen-by-twenty-foot hole in the wall. Flaming gasoline filled the War Relief Office on the seventy-eighth and seventy-ninth floors. Part of the fuselage crashed through the elevator shaft and plunged to the ground. One engine plowed through the seventy-eighth floor, crashed through the south wall and fell sixty-six stories to the roof of Henry Hering's penthouse apartment and studio at 10 West Thirty-third Street.

Summoned from the golf course to the scene, Hering found most of the

HE HELD HIS HAND ARM'S LENGTH BEFORE HIM AND PULLED THE TRIGGER

sculptures in his studio completely ruined. He found one project undamaged: metal models of his new design for "the golf club of the future." The *Times* reported: "He seemed more interested in the model golf clubs than in the works of art that had been shattered," or in the curious demises caused by the freak accident above.

Moe Berg graduated from Princeton, learned a dozen languages, served his country as a spy, maintained many scholarly interests, and was a professional baseball catcher. A nurse heard his last words: "How did the Mets do today?"

Socialite and part-time poet Fitzhugh Coyle Goldsborough objected to novelist David Graham Phillips' depiction of women. One Monday outside the Princeton Club, Goldsborough leaped in front of Phillips, cried "Now I have you!" and shot him six times.

Phillips lingered, calculating his odds. But he hardly had a sporting chance. "I could have won against two bullets, but not against six," he said. A few minutes later he folded.

Frank Lockhart won the Indy 500, but he was broke. All the money he won went into a new car, a Stutz Racer that could top the world land speed record of 206 miles an hour and make him rich from endorsements as the fastest man in the world.

His young wife didn't mind. She often donned overalls and helped Frank work on the Stutz. But his mother, a poor seamstress, was sick. She asked her son for money. Lockhart wired back, "I have the world by the horns. You'll never have to push a needle again."

He hit 225 miles an hour on the Daytona sands before a seashell caused a blowout that sent the Stutz tumbling down the beach. Lockhart flew out of the car and landed dead, not far from his young wife's feet.

Exercises the eminent historian Thomas Macaulay performed to Insure Intellectual Facility (and ward off senility):

* read one hundred pages of Schiller's *History of the War of the Netherlands* in the German;
* compared the average duration of the lives of archbishops, prime ministers, and lord chancellors;
* memorized the fourth act of *The Merchant of Venice* and the section of Lucretius in which nature mocks men who complain of mortality;
* read seven of Martial's twelve most famous books and memorized 360 of the best lines;
* studied the British peerage, the stock market, the revenue returns, the civil service estimates, and the clergy list;
* learned Italian; and
* read the novel he wrote thirty years before.

The exercises were successful. He wrote in his journal, "I am sensible of no intellectual decay—not the smallest." But the next day the ceiling in his bathroom collapsed just after he left it. He was so unnerved by this intimation of mortality that he died within the week.

DEADLY FIGHT IN THE JUNGLE.

5
Last Impressions

The famous Renaissance physician Andreas Vesalius felt the Count of Buren's pulse and advised him that he had five hours to live. The count didn't sulk. He made a will and confessed. Then he dressed in his best armor, put on the collar and coat of the Order of the Golden Fleece, and crowned himself with a hat, "in the Polish style." He summoned his friends, toasted the king, and gave an account of his largely forgettable life. As his time neared, be embraced Vesalius, went to his bed, fulfilled the famous doctor's prediction, and became a footnote in history.

A woman at a concert in London looked down at her feet and saw a naked man with his face covered by a cloak. No one else seemed to notice him, so she said she was ill and left. The next morning she learned that the night before a friend had slipped off a boat in the Thames and, tangled in his cloak, drowned.

I spent a shocking night," wrote Guy de Maupassant to a friend. "I have almost lost the use of speech, and my breathing is a sort of violent, rasping, horrible sound."

He consulted twelve doctors between 1889 and 1891, one of whom told him that he was suffering from neurasthenia—"It comes from intellectual overwork; every other writer and stockbroker is in your condition."

Another doctor told him to wash his face in salt solution.

"I am in my death agony," wrote de Maupassant. "I have a softening of the brain brought on by bathing my nostril with salt water. The salt has fermented in my brain, and every night my brains are dripping away through my nose and mouth in a sticky paste. . . ."

His agony lasted another year and a half, until he was carried off in a straitjacket after trying to rally his servant for a war against Prussia. On January 30, 1893, his friend Edmond de Goncourt wrote in his journal, "Maupassant begins to turn into an animal." Six months later, only 42 years old, the master of the short story died of syphilis.

Gallows Garb

Lady Jane Grey wore a black gown, a velvet-lined cape, and a black French hood for her execution.

A revolt threatened the rule of Henri I of Haiti. Paralysis kept him from leading his loyal troops, but as the rebels neared his palace the king bathed in hot rum and had servants rub him with flannel. Then he donned his full dress uniform —red coat with black revers, collar and cuffs, and red epaulets; white knee breeches and stockings; a shako trimmed with red silk lace, red braid, and red pompoms; and a gold badge bearing the royal arms. He walked toward his waiting troops but collapsed before he reached his horse.

Later, alone in his room, he dragged himself to his closet and wrapped himself in a white satin robe. Then he crawled back to his bed, loaded his pistol with a golden bullet, and shot it through his brain.

Rock and roll stars Buddy Holly and the Big Bopper died in a plane crash outside Mason City, Iowa, ending the Biggest Show of Stars tour. Holly had chartered the plane so he could go to Fargo, North Dakota, in time to have his shirts cleaned before the next show. After the crash, fans rushed to buy Holly's last song, "It Doesn't Matter Anymore."

The French aviatrix Mlle. Dutrieu didn't wear a corset, claiming that this "lessened the danger in case of a fall." The American flyer Harriet Quimby disagreed; she was always properly laced beneath her stylish flying outfit, complete with plum knickerbockers.

On July 2, 1912, more than a thousand spectators at Squantum Field near Boston watched Quimby take Bill Willard, the manager of the flying meet, up for a ride to the Boston Light. Her friends joked before she went up: "Throw Bill into the bay before you come back!"

At five hundred feet, her plane suddenly dipped. Willard fell out. The plane lurched again, and Harriet Quimby's plum-clad body fell into the shallow bay.

Some said her death proved that the airplane was too dangerous for women. Others claimed that a wire broke and a mechanic was at fault. Still others claimed that Willard was bankrupt and leaped from the plane to commit suicide. No one blamed Quimby's death on a faulty corset.

allows Garb

Earl Ferrers wore a white satin suit pinioned with a black silk sash (to match the silken noose) to his hanging at Tyburn in 1760.

Sam "Darling, You Send Me" Cooke picked up a twenty-two-year-old woman and brought her to his motel room. She got scared and ran away, taking all of his clothes with her. Clad only in an overcoat, Cooke gave chase. While the girl

hid in a telephone booth, he accused the motel clerk, fifty-five-year-old Bertha Lee Franklin, of hiding the girl. Bertha was no darling, but she sent Sam just the same. After Cooke allegedly slapped her twice, she reached for the gun she kept behind the counter. When the police arrived, they found three holes in the singer's body.

Charles Taze Russell believed that 1874 marked the beginning of the millennial age, during which Christ would return to govern the earth in person. He told the world about it through his publication *The Watchtower.* He also traveled all over the world preaching Christ's coming.

When his heart failed on a train in Texas, he begged, "Please wrap me in a Roman toga!" His assistants fashioned a toga around his body with Pullman sheets, and he died. It was Halloween, 1916.

One morning in March 1971 a car speeding down Cuthbert Road in Haddon Township, New Jersey, ran into a man pushing a shopping cart. Police found the corpse of the seventy-four-year-old indigent unremarkable, except that he wore four pairs of pants. The dead man also turned out to have a name. He was Winthrop Biddle, of *the* Biddles of Philadelphia, the family that ran the Bank of the United States.

Gallows Garb

King Charles I wore black satin clothes with a short velvet coat, pearl earrings, the decorations of George and the Garter, and carried a gold cane to his execution.

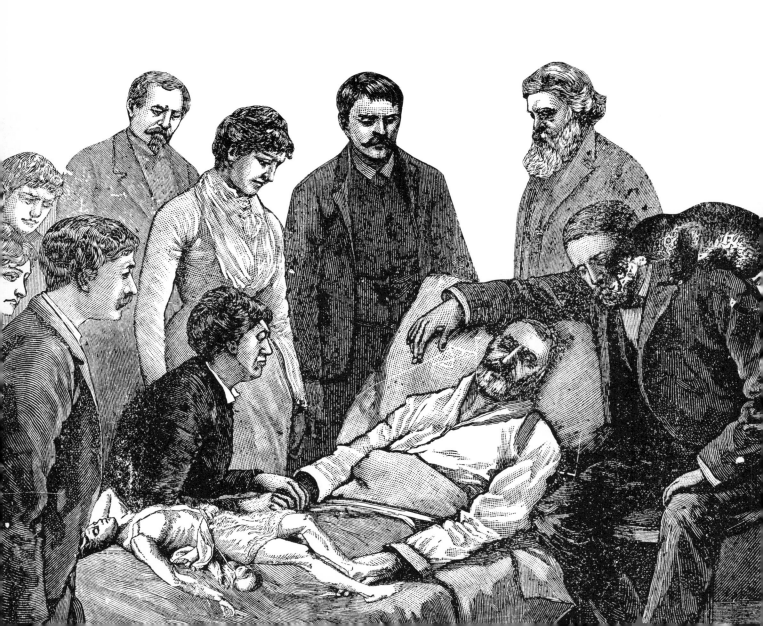

The poet Hart Crane paced the deck of the Mexico-to-New York steamer wearing his overcoat. His Guggenheim year in Mexico had produced one poem and one suicide attempt (he had drained a bottle of iodine and mercurochrome to no effect). Now he was returning home.

Crane stormed into the room of his traveling companion, told her how roughly sailors had treated him when he got drunk the night before, and bade her good-bye.

He walked to the promenade deck, took off his overcoat, and, clad only in pajamas, leaped into the calm blue sea off the Florida coast.

Gallows Garb

Marie Antoinette wore a morning gown with a muslin fichu crossed over her breast and a little white cap to her execution (all rudely ripped off afterward).

Cesare Borgia tried to succeed his father as pope, but his enemies got the prize. Cesare fled Italy and became a general for the king of Navarre. While besieging the castle of Viana a raiding party approached his lines. Cesare led an attacking charge, but none of his soldiers followed. Cesare fought to the finish. A blow in the armpits proved fatal.

The enemy stripped him "mother-naked," but one soldier couldn't bear to see one who was so famous so naked. He gave Cesare a private burial, putting a large rock over his penis.

Gallows Garb

In France back in 1386 a pig killed a child. Authorities deemed the murderer to be no pig but a devil. So they dressed the pig up in a man's suit of clothes and executed it.

6
Fleeting Expressions

Abram S. Hewitt, industrialist and ex-mayor of New York, took the oxygen tube out of his mouth and made an announcement from his hospital bed: "And now I am officially dead."

In a few minutes he was.

Father, here is your Louise. What are you thinking of as you lie here so happily?"

"I am going up. Come with me."

"Oh, I wish I could."

Bronson Alcott died. The next day Louisa May Alcott had a terrible headache. Before the doctor could determine whether she suffered from meningitis or apoplexy, her wish came true and up she went.

John Janeway, a young preacher, lay dying. He was not a taciturn man. As his hour neared he said:

"Oh, He is come! He is come! Oh, how sweet, how glorious is the blessed Jesus! He is altogether lovely! Oh my friends, stand still and wonder! How shall I speak the thousandth thought of His praises! Oh, for words to set forth..."

(to be continued)

Professor Halyburton, an eighteenth-century theologian, feared he would lose the power of speech on his deathbed. He told his friends that even if he couldn't speak, he would still try to give "a sign of triumph when I am near glory." At the end he couldn't speak. He lifted up his hands, clapped, and died.

66
Proust's
Last Beer

Y ou obstruct the way," was all Colonel Goodloe said when he met his political opponent in the Lexington post office.

"You spoke to me," noted Colonel Swope (who didn't like Goodloe's attempt to wrest the local leadership of the Republican party from him). "You insulted me."

Goodloe drew his dirk knife. Swope drew his Smith & Wesson .38. In what authorities hailed as "the greatest fight in the history of Kentucky," Goodloe stabbed Swope thirteen times, piercing his heart and nearly cutting off his hand. Swope shot Goodloe twice, tearing up his belly and setting his clothes on fire, so close was the gun barrel to the victim.

Swope dropped dead on the post office floor. Goodloe staggered to a doctor's office. The doctor put out the fire, but the wound was fatal. Thus one of the great short-winded political debates ended in a draw.

C omposer Henry Louis Reginald De Koven got word at a supper party in his honor that the third performance of his opera *Rip Van Winkle* was sold out. He dashed off a wire to his wife: BOX OFFICE VOX DEI — HURRAH. The real *vox Dei* delivered another message. Ten minutes after the good news, De Koven dropped dead.

T he Barcelona bus was overcrowded, so a passenger climbed onto the roof. Up there, he was alone with an empty coffin. When it started raining he climbed into the coffin to keep dry. Later, two more men climbed onto the roof of the bus. The man in the coffin heard their conversation. He asked them if it had stopped raining. Both men jumped off the bus. One died.

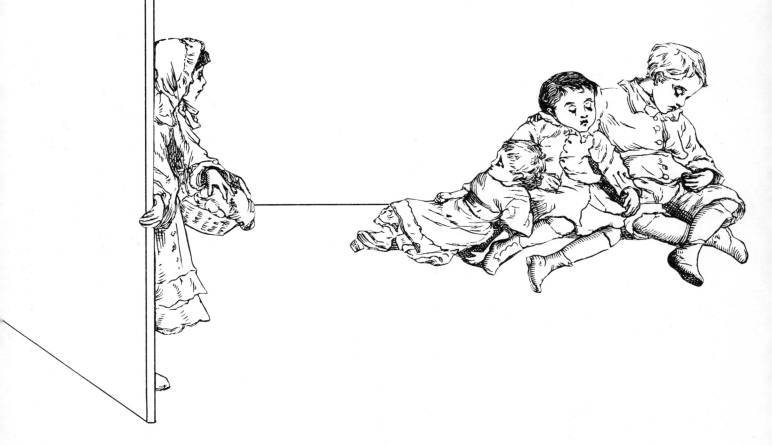

"Oh, pshaw!" said Grace, "they're all dead."

John Janeway's Last Words (continued)

(The young preacher, still dying, had more to say) "...a little of that excellency. But it is inexpressible. Oh, how excellent and glorious is the blessed Jesus! Come, my friends, look upon a dying man and wonder. Was there ever greater kindness. Was there ever more sensible manifestations of rich grace? Oh, why me, Lord? Why me? Surely this is akin to heaven. If this be dying it is sweet. Oh, that you did but see and feel what I do!..." **(to be continued)**

There was a lady in France who taught her parrot to express love for Napoleon. When Louis XVIII was on his way to Paris he stayed in that lady's house. She fled but left her parrot locked in a closet. In the night a cry— *"Vive l'empereur!"*— woke the king. Another cry — *Vive l'empereur!"* — outraged him. He summoned attendants who traced the treasonous cry to the closet and beat down the door. The parrot had time for a final *"Vive l'empereur!"* before they wrung its neck.

The poet Heinrich Heine fell in a heap in front of the limbless Venus de Milo in the Louvre courtyard. When passersby picked him up, he joked, "And the goddess did not stretch an arm to help me!"

He kept up the jokes for the remaining eight years of his paralysis and pain.

He chided friends for not calling: "If you miss the opportunity of seeing me, you will soon have to make the uncomfortable journey to Montmartre Cemetery, where I have already hired an apartment with a view overlooking eternity."

He heard about the rumor circulating in Paris that he had embraced religion: "If I could go out on crutches, do you know where I would go? Why, straight to church.

Where else should one go on crutches? Of course, if I could go without crutches, I should prefer to stroll along the gay boulevards and amuse myself in the Bal Mabille."

When a visitor asked if he was incurable, Heine replied, "No, I shall die someday."

Over the years friends tired of visiting the man with the decaying body but still-sharp mind. Heine joked about that: "Many a poet has survived his own immortality, but I, I survive my own death!"

When the end came, he didn't joke. He cried out, "Write! Write! Paper! Pencil!" The maid fetched them, but when he took hold of the pencil he shook with convulsions, dying without a punch line.

John Janeway's Last Words *(continued)*

"...Behold a dying man, more cheerful than you ever saw a man in health, and in the midst of his sweetest worldly enjoyments! Oh, sirs, worldly pleasures are poor, pitiful, sorry things when compared with this glory in my soul. This is the hour I have waited for. Praise is now my work, and I shall be engaged in that sweet enjoyment forever...."   *(to be continued)*

The poet Richard Savage was in prison for debt. He became ill with back and side pains. When he saw the jailer, he called out to him, "I have something to say to you, sir."

The jailer hurried to the sick man and leaned over to hear his words.

Savage shook his head and whispered, " 'Tis gone."

He spoke no more and died the next day.

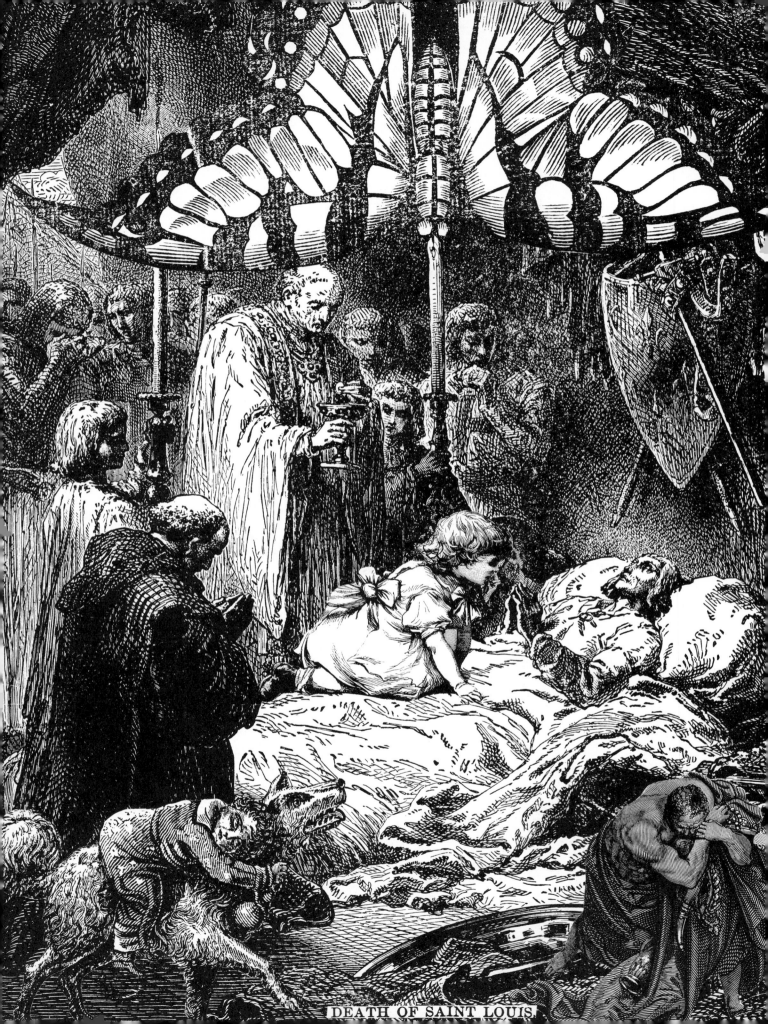

DEATH OF SAINT LOUIS

Balthazar Gerard shot William the Silent as the king left his midday meal. The Dutch dealt harshly with the assassin.

The executioner burned Gerard's right hand off with a hot iron, then took the flesh off his bones at six places with pincers. Gerard survived, say the chronicles, "never uttering so much as an 'ah, me.'"

As was the custom, the executioner then smashed the murder weapon to pieces in sight of the crowd and the condemned. A piece of pistol hit the executioner in the ear. Gerard smiled. And some say, when the executioner cut into Gerard's heart and flung it into his face, Gerard was still smiling.

John Janeway's Last Words *(continued)*

"...Oh help me to praise Him; I have nothing else to do. I have done with prayer; I have almost [!!] done with conversing with mortals. I shall soon behold Christ Himself, who died for me, and loved me, and washed me in His blood. I shall shortly be in eternity, singing the song of Moses, and the song of the Lamb..."

(to be continued)

Alfred Jarry, father of Theater of the Absurd, spent his last days in bed muttering *"Je cherche"* over and over. In a lucid moment he asked for a toothpick. His doctor rushed out and bought a package of toothpicks. Jarry grasped a toothpick, smiled, and died.

Cardiac malfunction, bronchopneumonia, and tainted crab meat conspired to cut short President Warren Harding's tour of the Northwest. Trying to cheer him as he rested in a San Francisco hotel, his wife read him a favorable assessment of his administration in the *Saturday Evening Post:* "A Calm Review of a Calm Man."

The story pleased Harding. "That's good. Read some more."

Then suddenly he twisted. His wife thought he was choking on chewing gum. She ran her fingers through his mouth. It wasn't chewing gum. He was having convulsions.

She ran from the room calling for doctors. Four rushed into the bedroom. Harding was calm. A doctor injected stimulants. Too calm. Harding was dead.

John Janeway's Last Words (continued)

"...I shall presently stand upon Mount Zion, with an innumerable company of angels, and the spirits of the just made perfect. I shall hear the voice of the multitudes, and be one amongst them who say 'Hallelujah! glory and honor and power unto the Lord our God.' My dear mother..."

(to be continued)

One night after dinner Oliver Goldsmith's friends wrote mock epitaphs for the eminent writer. Goldsmith's reply was his poem "Retaliation." When he took sick soon after writing it, the doctor offered no hope.

"Is your mind at ease?" asked the doctor.

"No, it is not," replied Goldsmith, and died.

Texas! Texas!" Sam Houston cried out at his end. But that wasn't his last word. His wife took the ring off his finger and showed it to all the Houston clan that had gathered around his deathbed.

"Honor," he read the inscription.

Henry David Thoreau's last days were filled with meaningful phrases. In answer to the question, "How does the opposite shore appear?" Thoreau answered, "One world at a time."

But those weren't his last words.

Asked if he had made peace with God, Thoreau answered, "I did not know we had ever quarreled."

But those weren't his last words.

His last words were: "Moose — Indian."

Father Matthew, Nikolai Gogol's spiritual adviser, was less than impressed with the second part of the novelist's *Dead Souls,* which was to be the *Purgatory* to the first part's *Inferno.* The father told Gogol to give up literary activity.

Late one night Gogol ordered his servant to bring his manuscript to the stove. As the boy stood aghast, Gogol burned it.

"Be content to pray!" warned Gogol.

The next day Tolstoy tried to encourage his colleague, reminding Gogol that he had burned manuscripts before only to rewrite them.

"Yes, yes, I can, I can. I have it all in my head!"

It stayed there. Gogol died ten days later.

Anthony J. Drexel III, a financier of the 1890s, showed one of the pistols in his gun collection to a friend. He said, "Here's one you've never seen before," and accidentally shot himself.

Under examination for witchcraft (after being stripped, isolated, and starved), one woman identified the four imps that aided her in sorcery. They were "Ile-mauzar, Pyewackett, Pecke in the Grown, and Griezzell Greedigutt." Since the witchfinder general found that they were names "which no mortal could invent," the woman was hung.

John Janeway's Last Words *(continued)*

"...brethren and sisters, farewell! I leave you for a short time. I commend you to God and to the world of His grace, which is able to build you up and to give you an inheritance among them which are sanctified. And now, dear Lord, my work is done. Come, Lord Jesus, come quickly."

And John Janeway died. Amen.

Noble Nods

"Oh, victory! Victory! How you distract my poor brain!"Admiral Horatio Nelson cried as he lay in his quarters after taking a fatal wound.

Captain Hardy returned from the deck with news that the battle was won and fourteen or fifteen ships captured.

"I bargained for twenty," Nelson replied.

Then he gave his last command: "Don't throw me overboard; you know what to do. Take care of my dear Lady Hamilton, Hardy. Kiss me, Hardy. Who is that?...God bless you Hardy....Thank God, I have done my duty."

As he died, the words "God and my country" were on his lips. (But some say in feverish pain he cried out, "Drink, drink! Fan, fan! Rub, rub!")

George II wasn't at his father's deathbed. He never made it to his own deathbed either. One fateful morning he rose at six as always, drank his chocolate, went to the toilet, collapsed, and died.

The seventeenth-century philosopher Michel de Montaigne, who made death his life's study, dreaded the thought of dying surrounded by "wailing women ... swooning friends ... whining servants ... physicians and preachers." Quoth Montaigne: "Happie is that death which takes all leasure from the preparations of such an equipage."

But when the philosopher was on his deathbed, he summoned his servants, the priest, and the physicians, and called in his friends to bid them good-bye. While rising to clasp a friendly hand, Montaigne died.

82
Proust's
Last Beer

The English writer Elizabeth Gaskell was also a student of death. Since her chief work was a biography of the short-lived Bronte family, she had to be. She had described the memorable deaths of four Brontes: Branwell who "resolved on standing up to die"; Emily who "to the last adhered tenaciously to her habits of independence and called for a doctor too late"; Anne who cried out "take courage, Charlotte, take courage"; and finally Charlotte who "saw her husband's woe-worn face" and rued, "I am not going to die, am I? He will not separate us. . . ."

When her own time came, Gaskell was in no position to face it à la Bronte, with either resolution, independence, compassion, or pathos. While having tea with friends, "*quite* suddenly, without a moment's warning, in the midst of a sentence," she dropped dead.

Charlemagne died of natural causes at the age of seventy-two and bequeathed his heirs a vast kingdom. His heirs failed to match Charlemagne for dignity on the throne — or on the deathbed. Louis the Debonair starved to death. Charles the Bald was poisoned by his physician. Poison also killed Louis the Stutterer. Charles of Aquitaine died of a head wound received while in costume trying to scare a lord named Albuin. Louis III took after a pretty girl in Tours, was thrown from his horse, and died. Carloman died of a spear wound after a servant mistook him for a wild boar. Charles the Fat died of grief and poison. Charles the Simple died in prison. Louis the Stranger died of bruises after a hunting accident. And the runts of the line, Lotharius and Louis the Lazy, were both poisoned by their wives.

Captain Bucky O'Neill led the Rough Riders down a sunken country lane. As bullets whizzed by, Bucky stopped and lit a cigarette.

"For God's sake, Captain," cried a sergeant, "get under cover!"

"Don't worry, Sergeant," Bucky boasted. "The Spanish bullet isn't molded that will kill me."

A bullet ripped open Bucky's throat, cutting short the boasting, and Bucky.

A bullet didn't kill Old Abe the Eagle. After serving as the mascot of the 8th Wisconsin in thirty-six Civil War battles, he only lost a few feathers. One Rebel general averred, "I would rather take that eagle than a whole brigade!"

In March 1881 a cold wave gripped Madison, Wisconsin. Although his touring days were over—he had made $80,000 as an exhibit at the the Centennial Fair in Philadelphia—Abe liked to get a breath of air. But his keeper wouldn't let Abe out in the bitter cold that would surely kill him. Abe squawked and squawked. The cold spell didn't break. After a week Abe stopped squawking and stopped eating, too. He grew weak. His keeper rocked Old Abe in his arms as he died.

When his memory began slipping Immanuel Kant made a syllabus each night for the next day, but the philosopher started forgetting where he had put the syllabus. "That I am becoming so infirm," he said, "probably arises from a revolution in the strata of the air which occurred several years ago." (He was referring to 1796 when, according to a Swiss scientist's paper, a change in the electrical condition of

the atmosphere caused a large number of cats to die in Europe. Kant ascribed all illness, except that caused by beer, to atmospheric conditions.)

In his seventy-ninth year he collapsed in the street. He had unpleasant dreams and complained of assassins and childhood melodies resounding in his ears. Then he gorged himself on English cheese, and had a stroke the next day.

He could no longer write. On February third he stopped eating. On the fifth he had guests to dinner, but he didn't eat or speak. On the seventh he had guests but stayed in bed. On the eleventh he couldn't talk. His servant asked if he recognized him. Kant gave him a kiss. On the twelfth he drank water, said, "It is well," and died.

As for atmospheric conditions, there was one small cloud in the sky. Town tradition says it was Kant's soul flying to heaven.

Secretly, in my heart of hearts, I still hope to be able to make something of myself," composer Franz Schubert confided to a friend. "But who can do anything after Beethoven?"

Delirious in the final stages of typhoid fever, Schubert raved, "I implore you to transfer me to my room, not to leave me here, in this corner under the earth; do I deserve no place above the earth?"

His brother assured him he was in his own bed.

"No, it is not true," Schubert cried. "Beethoven does not lie here."

They buried him next to Beethoven.

The Scottish anthropologist Sir James George Frazer reports in *The Golden Bough* that an ancient African tribe, the Shilluks, believed that their god Nyakang resided in their king. If the king grew weak, then Nyakang grew weak, and cattle and crops died. To forestall that catastrophe the Shilluk priests executed the king whenever one of his wives complained of his weakness. The mode of execution was to isolate the king in a walled-up hut with no food or water, and with a young virgin to share his doom.

Once, Frazer claims, the starving king survived his companion for many days, and "was so distressed by the stench of her putrefying body that he shouted to the people, never again to let a king die in such prolonged and exquisite agony."

The Shilluks obeyed. The next king died alone.

When George Washington caught a cold, his rule was to do nothing and "let it go as it came." In the winter of 1799 he caught a bad cold. Washington might do nothing, but his doctors found it hard to watch the hero die without trying some cures.

But after a drink of molasses, vinegar, and butter; bleeding; sal volatile on the throat; a foot bath in warm water; a blister of Spanish fly on the throat; bleeding; steam from a kettle of vinegar and water; a drink of sage tea and vinegar; bleeding; a dish of calomel and tartar emetic; plasters on his legs and a soft poultice of wheat bran on the throat, the general gave his last command: "Do not let my body be put in the vault in less than two days after I'm dead."

Parson Weems, Washington's first biographer and creator of the cherry tree legend, gave a more elevating description of the passage: "Swift as angel's wings the brightening saint ascended; while voices more than human were warbling through the happy region, and hymning the great procession toward the gates of heaven...."

Only Bianchon can save me," the French novelist Honoré de Balzac said on his deathbed.

How could he resist calling for the doctor of his novels? When Père Goriot was

Death surprising a pair of lovers

dying, Bianchon, then only a student, managed with another student to change the dying man's dirty linen. Goriot's last words to the young men were "My angels!"

Balzac's death was as messy as Goriot's. Victor Hugo saw him: "His face was purple, almost black. . . . An intolerable odor rose from the bed. I drew back the coverlet and took Balzac's hand. It was damp with sweat. I pressed it, but he did not return the pressure."

The doctor used a hundred leeches on Balzac, employed in three shifts, to try to ease the dropsical swelling. Gangrene set in, and all the doctor could do was open the windows and set bowls of phrenicated water around the bed to try to kill the smell.

No one heard Balzac cry out to the angels; he died alone.

In 1665, when four-year-old Carlos became king of Spain, the French ambassador reported, "The doctors do not foretell a long life." The French and Austrians began angling for the Spanish succession.

Carlos came of age and married. But he was sterile, so the French and Austrians continued to scheme.

In 1696 the English ambassador wrote, "Carlos swallows all he eats whole, for his nether jaw stands so much out that his two rows of teeth cannot meet; to compensate which, he has a prodigious wide throat, so that a gizzard of liver passes down whole, and his weak stomach not being able to digest it, he voids in the same manner."

In early 1698 the ambassador reported that the king had only a few weeks to live. By mid 1698 ". . . his eyes bag, the lids are as red as scarlet and the rest of his face is a greenish yellow." Four days later the king had fits. There was no hope, according to the ambassador. The king recovered.

In 1699 he relapsed. The French reported the king was dead. There was rioting in the streets, but two weeks later the king looked better than ever.

In September, 1700 the king got so sick that doctors put freshly killed pigeons on his head to keep him warm. The king became mute, then went into a sweat. On November 1, at 2:48 P.M., he died.

At last Europe could begin the War of the Spanish Succession.

Her rheumatism, Bright's disease, and bad heart, according to her doctor, would have killed most people, but Madame Blavatsky, guru of the Theosophists, lived on, until influenza struck.

Her disciples kept a round-the-clock vigil, giving her a tablespoon of brandy every two hours. She tried to play solitaire, but the cards were too heavy. She sorted through her papers, burning some. The doctor admired her courage.

"I do my best, doctor," she whispered. With her waning strength she rolled her last cigarette and handed it to the doctor.

Two more days and nights she sat in her chair propped up with pillows, surrounded by disciples waiting for the last words of the one who had received and passed on so many Truths from the Beyond.

She died without a murmur.

England saw the handwriting on the wall. Nell became pale; Nell had to rest during her chores; Nell began hanging around graveyards; Nell spent whole days lying on a couch. Readers of the serial *The Old Curiosity Shop* inundated its author, Charles Dickens, with pleas that Little Nell be spared. But in the next episode of the story Dickens wrote:

. . . She seemed a creature fresh from the hand of God, and waiting for the breath of life; not one who had lived and suffered death.

Her couch was dressed with here and there some winter berries and green leaves, gathered in a spot she had been used to favor. "When I die, put me near something that has loved the light, and had the sky above it always." Those were her words.

She was dead. Dear gentle, patient, noble Nell was dead. . . .

The actor Macready wrote in his diary: "I have never read printed words that gave me so much pain." The Irish politician O'Connell shouted, "He should not have killed her!" and threw the story out a window. The first cry to ships coming to New York was "Is Little Nell dead?" And New York wept at the reply.

he Flower that once has blown for ever dies.

8
Swan Songs

Jack Zuta crossed Al Capone. Zuta fled to a resort hotel on a lake near Milwaukee. While he lounged in the hotel ballroom, five of Capone's men entered quietly. Rat-a-tat, rat-a-tat, sixteen times. Zuta's body slammed into a coin-operated piano. The tune that resulted: "Good for You, Bad for Me."

I must have taken poison. I cannot get this idea out of my mind. . . . I have the flavor of death on my tongue — I taste death."

So Wolfgang Amadeus Mozart wrote to friends. His wife told him he was ill from working too hard on the requiem that a patron had commissioned. She took the score away. Mozart felt better. Soon he was well enough to work on the requiem again.

He had a relapse. His hands swelled. Paralysis crippled his body. He kept on working. His wife let him. They needed the money.

One afternoon he sang the requiem with friends. As he sang the "Lacrimosa" he burst into tears. That night he joked: "Did I not say that I was writing the requiem for myself?"

The doctor came and applied cold bandages. Shuddering and delirious, Mozart blew out his cheeks, imitating the drum and trumpet parts of the unfinished requiem. Around midnight he sat up in bed, opened his eyes wide, then lay back down, faced the wall, and slept. An hour later he died.

The composer Pietro Guglielmi wanted to find out how high castrati could sing. He prodded the young castrato Luca Fabbris higher and higher until Fabbris collapsed on stage and died.

96
Proust's
Last Beer

Whenever composer Jerome Kern was about to leave his home in Beverly Hills to go to New York, he sat at the piano and played a few bars of "Ol' Man River" for good luck. One time he didn't, and he felt uneasy.

His third day in town he left the Hotel St. Regis to do some shopping. On the corner of Fifty-seventh Street and Park Avenue he collapsed. Finding no local address on his person, police took him to the hospital on Welfare Island where they always took unknowns and indigents.

Someone in the crowd recognized Kern and alerted theater people. Oscar Hammerstein rushed to Welfare Island. He tried to revive Kern by singing "Ol' Man River" in his ear, but it was too late. Kern never regained consciousness and died a few days later.

A friend found songwriter Stephen Foster naked on the floor of his Bowery room. Blood oozed from a neck wound that he apparently got from a broken water pitcher. Foster was so weak "his eyelids kept fluttering."

Help came too late, and a few days later he died in a hospital. He was thirty-seven. His only possessions were thirty-eight cents, and a bag which contained these words penciled on a scrap of paper: "Dear friends and gentle hearts."

After the First Engineering Battalion bridged the Tone River, General Hayashi left. Bugler Tsuruoka sounded a call in his honor. Halfway through he realized he was playing the wrong call. He hung himself later that day to atone for the wrong tune at the Tone.

98
Proust's
Last Beer

The day before, she had fainted after every piece she sang. But three thousand people paid to see the final concert of the Manchester Festival, and Maria Malibran knew they had come to hear her. She forgot about the recent fall she'd had off a runaway horse, she forgot her pregnancy, she forgot her fainting spells, she sang. She even sang in a *bel canto* duel with Maria Caterina Caradori-Allan.

As the divas elaborated on the duet *"Vanne, se alberghi in patto"* from Mercandante's *Andronico*, the audience went wild. They called for an encore.

Malibran appealed for rest, but the crowd wanted more. She told the conductor, Sir George Smart, "If I go on again, it will be the death of me."

"You need only withdraw and I will apologize to the audience," he replied.

She couldn't watch her rival sing alone. She sang, and the roars of the house bestowed the victory upon her. Offstage she collapsed into the arms of Caradori-Allan. Nine days later, she died.

After listening to the soundtrack for *Buried Alive in the Blues* Janis Joplin had two vodkas and orange juice, went home, and died of an overdose of heroin.

As poet William Blake's end neared, his face brightened and he sang about heaven. His wife admired the songs. Blake cried out, "My beloved, they are not mine. No! They are not mine!"

A neighbor who was there told the world, "I have been at the death, not of a man, but of a blessed angel."

Arthur Rubinstein played the Chopin sonata with the Funeral March at Count Strogonoff's house. He thought everyone had retired, but when he reached the trio he heard sobs coming from behind a chair. It was the count crying, "It is over, it is over. The march told me it is over."

The count died a few weeks later.

At a dinner party a friend asked Rubinstein to play the Funeral March. He refused, explaining that the march was too long to play at a social occasion. The friend insisted. Rubinstein played. Listening intently, the friend was soon in tears. Two weeks later he died in a car accident.

Rubinstein stopped playing Chopin's Funeral March for friends.

A Cadillac sped north from Nashville on New Year's Eve, 1955. Country music star Hank Williams celebrated alone in the back seat. He took nips of whiskey and a little chloral hydrate, a soporific, for the long ride to his next concert in Canton, Ohio.

Outside Rutledge, Tennessee, a cop stopped the Cadillac. He wrote out a ticket for speeding and mentioned that the man in the back seat looked dead. Not until the Puroil Gas Station in Oak Ridge, West Virginia, did the driver check to see why Hank slept so soundly.

With the news of Hank's death, sales of his last record "I'll Never Get Out of this World Alive" skyrocketed.

Eight days after being shot by an assassin, President William McKinley seemed to be on the way to recovery. He had an appetite and ate a bowl of chicken broth, a small piece of toast, and a cup of coffee.

Suddenly he felt sick. Doctors thought it was indigestion. McKinley knew it

wasn't. He whispered the words of his favorite hymn to his wife, "Nearer My God to Thee . . ." and died.

An autopsy showed it wasn't indigestion. It was gangrene and pancreatic failure.

Dr. Arne, an eighteenth-century English composer, was talking about music with the singer Vernon. Arne tried to illustrate a point by singing part of an air. He was very weak and his feeble voice sang a song that became fainter and fainter until the composer breathed no more.

Lincoln Beachey, a parakeet belonging to the author of this book, began having convulsions in the afternoon. They continued into the night. Death seemed so certain that the author played Verdi's *Requiem* on his stereo. The bird struggled on. The author played Elgar's *Death of Gerontus* and the last act of Puccini's *Madame Butterfly*. Still the bird struggled on. During the "Ode to Joy" of Beethoven's Ninth Symphony, the convulsions stopped.

Over the next few days Beachey-bird regained his strength but was unable to say any of the many words he had learned: "I like Ike," "Franz Schubert," "Mozart," "Peep, peep, peep," etcetera.

One morning the author found the fird stretched out pitifully in his cage. The author took the bird in his hand. The bird cried, "Peep!"

It was his last; he was dead.

Later that day the author played Mahler's *Kindertoten Lieder.*

The doctor asked John Wesley if he was in pain, and the Methodist leader sang the hymn "All Glory to God in the Sky." Then his strength failed. He asked for paper and pen but couldn't write. Someone offered to take dictation. Wesley cried out, "God is with us!" and broke into the hymn "I'll Praise My Maker While I've Breath." He got up and sat in a chair. Looking nearly dead, he sang "To Father, Son, and Holy Ghost," until he weakened. He murmured, "Now we have done—let us all go." But no one did because he stayed.

Most of the night he led the faithful in prayer. Once he cried out, "Farewell, farewell!" but still lingered.

In the morning more admirers came to his bedside. He tried to kiss his sister-in-law, and sang, "We thank Thee, O Lord, for these all Thy mercies. . . ."

A little later he sang out, "The clouds drop fatness!" Then he cried, "The God of Jacob is our refuge!" He led some more prayers, and most of that night he kept trying to recite a psalm but could only repeat, "I'll praise—I'll praise!"

The next morning he muttered, "Farewell," and finally died.

Henry Murger, who wrote the story that became the plot for Puccini's opera *La Bohème*, actually lived through the privations described in his story. Even when he became wealthy he never regained his health. He died only thirteen years after the real-life model for Mimi. Suffering great pain, sleepless nights, and fever, at his end sweat poured down his face and his breathing rattled. He said his last words:

"No music, no noise . . . no Bohemia," and died.

9
Appointments with Death

On her deathbed, surrounded by friends, Lady Astor asked, "Am I dying or is this my birthday?"

Shortly before explorer Sir Henry Stanley died of pleurisy, he heard Big Ben strike the hour.

"What is that?" he asked his wife.

"Four o'clock," she told him.

"Four o'clock? How strange. So that is the time! How strange."

3 Months Early

An ad in the *Kankakee Daily Republican* of June 14, 1918, reported this testimonial from Horace Greeley Ford:

> My kidney acted irregularly, the secretions were highly colored and hard to pass. I had severe pains in the back of my head too. I bought two boxes of Doan's Kidney Pills and they have greatly benefitted me and put my kidneys in order.

Investigators for the American Medical Association checked up on Ford's testimonial and found that Ford had died on March 19, 1918—three months earlier.

3 Days Early

Queen Caroline, wife of George II, was born on a Wednesday, married on a Wednesday, was crowned on a Wednesday, and, after an operation for her rupture failed, expected to die on a Wednesday.

One night she got a rattle in her throat. She knew it couldn't be a death rattle because it was only Sunday.

"I have got an asthma," she declared. "Open the window."

It wasn't asthma.

"Pray!" she cried out, and died.

1 Day Early

The most famous photograph of Calamity Jane shows her standing next to Wild Bill Hickok's big tombstone. So when she was "sicker 'n hell's fire" and dying, she asked the prospector spoon-feeding her whiskey the date; knowing she was fading fast, he was kind enough to reply, "August second."

"Twenty-seventh anniversary of Wild Bill's murder," remembered Jane with satisfaction.

She died within the hour.

Actually, it was only August 1. But if you ever see Calamity Jane, don't tell her that.

1 Hour Early

Edward Herbert, a British divine known only for his feeble opposition to the famous philosopher Hobbes, asked what time it was. When told, he stated, "An hour hence I shall depart." Time mocked his deathbed prediction as easily as Hobbes had mocked his philosophy. With fifty-nine minutes left to go, Herbert rolled over and died.

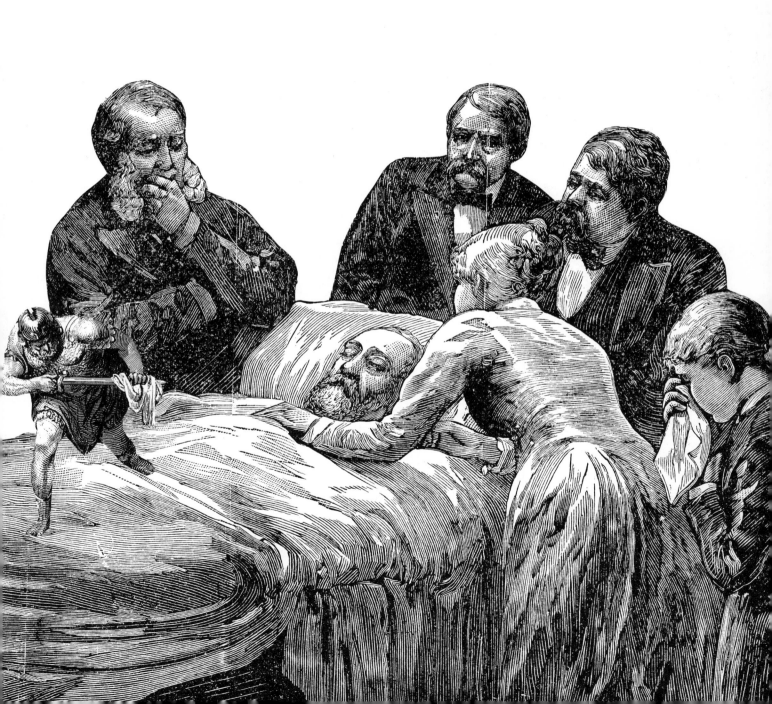

DRUIDS OFFERING HUMAN SACRIFICE.

11 Minutes Early

Even though he had a pain in his side, pianist Louis Moreau Gottschalk performed for the packed house in Rio de Janeiro. He opened the concert with his own composition "Morte." After six bars he fell to the floor.

He battled pain and fever for three weeks. In his final delirium he sang, made speeches in English, Spanish, and French, and called for his family. In a lucid moment he told a nurse, "Get a lawyer to take down my will. I'll die when the clock strikes four in the morning."

The lawyer was there at 1:00 A.M., but Gottschalk was unconscious. He died at 3:49 A.M.

Young

The poet Heinrich Heine didn't like the composer Vincenzo Bellini.

"You are a genius, Bellini," Heine told the composer during a dinner party, "but you will pay for your great gifts with a premature death. All the great geniuses died very young, like Raphael and like Mozart."

"Don't say that, for the love of God!" Bellini cried, and shook his hand in the prescribed way to ward off evil.

"Let's hope, my friend," Heine didn't shut up, "that in fact you are not a genius. The good fairies gave you a thousand other gifts . . . the face of a cherub, the candor of a boy, and the stomach of a stork. Let us hope that the evil fairy didn't intrude among those good ones and ruin everything by stirring in genius."

The hostess of that dinner invited the two men to another dinner so she could reconcile them, but Bellini sent a note saying he was sick. After battling a fever for fourteen days he died, only thirty-four years old.

n Time

Ethel Lynn Beers told friends that she had a premonition that death would come once her poems were collected and published. On October 10, 1879, *All Quiet Along the Potomac and Other Poems* by Ethel Lynn Beers was published. On October 11, 1879, she perished.

o Beat the Clock

When the health of his brother King George IV declined, William gargled every morning and wore galoshes to thwart chills. He wanted to be king.

When King William IV, popularly known as Silly Billy, began to grow weak, he kept his eyes on the calendar. He wanted to live past May 24, the day Princess Victoria came of age, so that the duchess of Kent, whom he abhorred, would not become regent even for a day. He lived past May 24.

Very ill, he still looked forward to celebrating another Waterloo Day, June 18. He told the doctors, "Try if you cannot tinker me up to last out that day."

On June 18 he was very weak. June 19, he was unconscious. At 2:30 A.M., June 20, he died. After the autopsy, doctors were amazed he lasted so long. "His lungs were turgid with blood, the heart valves ossified, the liver enlarged, and the spleen double its normal size."

A Little Late

Henry Keller, twenty-two, a clerk in a Newark bakery, grew despondent because his wife of four months, Florence, had fallen in love with his brother Ed. At 11:45 P.M. Henry began giving himself doses of gas as he sat at his desk. He wrote:

LAST HOUR OF BOOTH.

This would be a real opportunity for an essay on "How It Feels To Sentence Oneself to Die," but who cares. So many darned suicides have an idea that the rest of the world is going to be interested in their theories — horse feathers! They are interested in the prohibition question, or the price of eggs — in pies. . . .

There's two perfectly good pies here that some one might eat. . . .

I'll bet Florence and Ed are having uneasy dreams now. . . . My head is hot. I'm perspiring and shaky, brain is still clear though. Wonder who will add up the pies tomorrow. . . .

Hope I pass out by 2 A.M.

Gee I love you so much Florence. It's now 2:15 A.M. I feel very tired — a bit dizzy. I have the gas nozzle plastered to my face but disconnected from the gas jet. It's quite uncomfortable, damn it. My brain is very clear, I can see that my hand is shaking — it is hard to die when one is young. Now I wish oblivion would hurry —

The last words were written in a broad shaky scrawl.

1 Hour Late

The mystic Jakob Böhme was dying of gastric disease. As the end neared he heard music that no one else heard. He asked for the time and his son told him it was two.

"My time is not yet," said the visionary mystic. "Three hours hence is my time." He died at six.

2 Days Late

At noon fourteen-year-old Elizabeth Cunningham asked the doctor how long she had to live. The doctor told her she might last until eight.

"Oh, that is good news indeed!" she exclaimed, anxious to meet her Maker.

She counted the hours. When the clock struck seven she chortled, "Another hour and then."

She lasted the night. She even looked better in the morning. When the doctor asked how she felt, she answered, "Truly happy. If this be dying, it is a pleasant thing to die."

During the day her parents tried to get her to struggle on. Wouldn't she want to live if the Lord restored her to perfect health?

"Not for all the world," she replied. Or when she really felt like dying, "Not for a thousand worlds."

The next day, long overdue, death rewarded its enthusiast.

1 Month Late

"This month is deadly for fat people," said Pope Alexander VI in July 1503, as he watched the funeral of his brother Juan Borgia (who, most say, was poisoned by Alexander's son Cesare). But the portly pope survived July.

On August 17 the pope contracted a fatal fever (some say from Cesare's poison). The next day he died.

1,431 Days Late

The German poet Novalis fell in love with a twelve-year-old girl. All agreed that she was an angel. Novalis married her. She became very ill. While Novalis was off

studying medicine so he could cure his wife, she died before reaching her sixteenth birthday.

Novalis began a journal of his grief. In her memory he observed a different calendar:

> 32nd day after Sophie's death — I read Wilhelm Meister. . . .
> 43rd day after Sophie's death — in the morning I wept bitterly. After dinner again. The whole day her memory seemed sanctified to me.

1,431 days after Sophie's death, Novalis died.

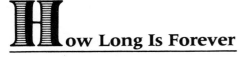

How Long Is Forever

"I am just going outside and may be some time," Captain Oates told his comrades in the fatal Scott Polar Expedition. He crawled out into the raging blizzard never to be seen again.

10
The Zodiac of Death
and Handy Index

Aries
March 21 to April 19

If you die under the sign of Aries you will have been an innovative and imaginative person almost to the point of seeming crazy to many. Your creativity put you in the White House, or a bullet in your back. Or you may have just made frankfurters. You were well dressed and very creative with rags. In romance, you loved them and left them. Some famous people who died under the sign of Aries are:

March 21   Pocahantas, who died in 1617

March 22   Johann Wolfgang von Goethe, 1832

March 23   Peter Lorre, 1964

March 24   Jules Verne, 1894

March 25   King Faisal, 1975

March 26   Ludwig von Beethoven, 1827 (see page 13) and Old Abe the Eagle, 1881 (see page 83)

March 27   Yuri Gagarin, 1968

March 28   Dwight David Eisenhower, 1969

March 29   Gustavus Swift, 1903

March 30   Beau Brummell, 1840 (in rags)

March 31   Charlotte Bronte, 1855 (see page 82) and Ebenezer Butterick, 1903 (inventor of the tissue-paper dress pattern)

April 1   Scott Joplin, 1917

April 2   Samuel F. B. Morse, 1872

April 3   Jesse James, 1882
April 4   Oliver Goldsmith, 1774 (see page 74)
April 5   Chauncey M. Depew, 1928 (who said "I get my exercise acting as pallbearer to my friends who exercised.")
April 6   Raphael, 1520
April 7   Henry Ford, 1947
April 8   Elisha Otis, 1861 (ride an elevator)
April 9   Francis Bacon, 1626 (see page 33)
April 10   Former King Zog of Albania, 1961
April 11   Luther Burbank, 1926
April 12   FDR, 1945 (see page 12) and Clara Barton, 1912 (see page 41)
April 13   Diamond Jim Brady, 1917
April 14   Richard Hickock and Perry Smith, 1965 (read *In Cold Blood*)
April 15   Wallace Beery, 1949
April 16   Edna Ferber, 1968
April 17   Ben Franklin, 1790
April 18   Albert Einstein, 1955
April 19   Charles Darwin, 1882

Taurus
April 20 to May 20

If you die under the sign of Taurus you will have been the type of person who created illusions and then stripped them off layer by layer, sometimes leaving an oxymoron like "Tragedy is the soul of humor" behind. You left a sex life clouded in mystery but had a complete dossier about everybody else's sex life. Although you tried to play it safe you got runs in your nylons. Living on a stage you thought nothing of going from Here to Eternity. Some famous people who died under the sign of Taurus are:

April 20	Henry Chadwick, 1908 (father of baseball)
April 21	Mark Twain, 1910
April 22	James Forrestal, 1949 (first U.S. secretary of defense—a suicide)
April 23	William Shakespeare, 1616
April 24	Willa Cather, 1947
April 25	Frank Lockhart, 1928 (see page 51)
April 26	Gypsy Rose Lee, 1970, and Hart Crane, 1932 (see page 62)
April 27	Edward R. Murrow, 1965, and Ralph Waldo Emerson, 1882
April 28	Josiah Strong, 1916 (who started the "Safety First" movement)
April 29	Wallace Hume Carothers, 1937 (inventor of nylon—a suicide)
April 30	Edouard Manet, 1883
May 1	John Dryden, 1700
May 2	J. Edgar Hoover, 1972
May 3	Bruce Cabot, 1972 (see *King Kong*)

May 4   Moe Howard, 1975 (last of the Three Stooges)

May 5   James A. Bland, 1911 (sang "Oh, Dem Golden Slippers")

May 6   Henry David Thoreau, 1862 (see page 77)

May 7   Lurleen Wallace, 1968, and the *Lusitania*, 1916

May 8   Madame Blavatsky, 1891 (see page 90)

May 9   James Jones, 1977

May 10   Big Daddy Lipscomb, 1963 (see page 45)

May 11   Gustav Mahler, 1911

May 12   Erich von Stroheim, 1957

May 13   Gary Cooper, 1961, and Dan "Hoss" Blocker, 1972

May 14   August Strindberg, 1912

May 15   Emily Dickinson, 1886

May 16   James Agee, 1955

May 17   Sandro Botticelli, 1510

May 18   Jacob Coxey, 1951 (who led his army in 1894)

May 19   Ogden Nash, 1971

May 20   Charles Francis Adams, Jr. 1915

Gemini

May 21 to June 21

If you die under the sign of Gemini you will have been a hero to some, a traitor to others—good with an ax but difficult to convict. Your life made a good plot for a movie, and as for death — why not Inside Heaven? You gloried in dispensing machine gun bullets and dimes, anything to help the miserable folk. One thing is certain, you don't get around much anymore

May 21	Audie Murphy, 1971
May 22	Victor Hugo, 1885
May 23	Bonnie and Clyde, 1934, and John D. Rockefeller, 1937
May 24	Duke Ellington, 1974
May 25	Moses G. Farmer, 1893 (inventor of the "self-exciting dynamo")
May 26	Samuel Pepys, 1703
May 27	Robert Ripley, 1949 (Believe It or Not)
May 28	Noah Webster, 1843
May 29	John Gunther, 1970, W.S. Gilbert, 1911 (see page 45), and Moe Berg, 1972 (see page 51)
May 30	Milton Bradley, 1911 (first board game: "The Checkered Game of Life")
May 31	(Franz) Joseph Haydn, 1809
June 1	Lizzie Borden, 1927
June 2	Lou Gehrig, 1941

June 3   Stephen Douglas, 1861 (see page 41), and Nicolas Appert, 1841 (inventor of the bouillon cube)

June 4   Casanova, 1798

June 5   O. Henry, 1910

June 6   Carl Jung, 1961

June 7   Jean Harlow, 1937, and Edwin Booth, 1893 (see page 41)

June 8   George Sand, 1876, and Thomas Paine, 1819

June 9   Charles Dickens, 1870, and Carry Nation, 1911

June 10   Miss Fitzsimmons, 1893 (the battling kangaroo boxer)

June 11   Belle Boyd, 1900 (the Confederate spy)

June 12   Saul Alinsky, 1972

June 13   Martin Buber, 1965

June 14   Benedict Arnold, 1801

June 15   James K. Polk, 1849

June 16   Brian Piccolo, 1970

June 17   Edward Burne-Jones, 1898

June 18   Maxim Gorky, 1936

June 19   Julius and Ethel Rosenberg, 1953

June 20   Silly Billy, 1837 (see page 112)

June 21   Inigo Jones, 1652

Cancer

June 22 to July 21

If you die under the sign of Cancer you will have been a deductive reasoner who still had many close shaves. Sex was big in your life. In the South you lusted after men with moustaches. In New York you liked girls naked on swings. And in Paris you soaked in a tub until she came. You miss Friday, and if you died on the fourth, you were a president of the United States! On the third, you were a rock star! You never bargained you would get over the rainbow so soon.

June 22	Judy Garland, 1969
June 23	William S. Hart, 1946
June 24	Grover Cleveland, 1908
June 25	Stanford White, 1906
June 26	Ford Maddox Ford, 1939
June 27	Earl Browder, 1973
June 28	Fatty Arbuckle, 1933 (died laughing)
June 29	Jayne Mansfield, 1967, and Elizabeth Barrett Browning, 1861 (see page 8)
June 30	Lee De Forest, 1961 (listen to radio)
July 1	Captain Bucky O'Neill, 1898 (see page 83)
July 2	Ernest Hemingway, 1961
July 3	Brian Jones, 1969 (by the pool), and Jim Morrison, 1971 (in the tub)
July 4	John Adams, 1826, Thomas Jefferson, 1826, and James Monroe, 1831

July 5	Ben Alexander, 1969 (watch a *Dragnet* rerun)
July 6	Guy de Maupassant, 1893 (see page 55), and William Faulkner, 1962
July 7	Arthur Conan Doyle, 1930
July 8	Vivien Leigh, 1967
July 9	Zachary Taylor, 1850 (see page 16), and King Camp Gillette, 1932 (shave)
July 10	Paul Morphy, 1884 (chess victim), and Henri II of France, 1559 (joust victim)
July 11	Jelly Roll Morton, 1941
July 12	No biggies died this day. Can you fill the bill?
July 13	Arnold Schoenberg, 1951 (always apprehensive of the number 13, he died on a Friday)
July 14	Anton Chekhov, 1904 (see page 13)
July 15	Jean Paul Marat, 1793
July 16	Samuel Insull, 1938
July 17	John Coltrane, 1967
July 18	Horatio Alger, 1899
July 19	Margaret Fuller, 1850
July 20	Paul Valéry, 1945
July 21	Basil Rathbone, 1967

Leo

July 22 to August 21

If you die under the sign of Leo you will have lived a life full of flights, whether of fancy, fugues, or flyballs. In politics, whiskers, coonskins, and poker-playing pals got you in trouble. When others took offense at your roaring good humor, you got very depressed. When you died you were a victim. Unless you had a friend named Alice, members of the opposite sex played a great role in your life. Either she gave you ten kids, or you gave her an ear.

July 22   Carl Sandburg, 1967, and John Roebling, 1869 (see page 33)

July 23   Eddie Rickenbacker, 1973

July 24   Martin Van Buren, 1862

July 25   Samuel Taylor Coleridge, 1834

July 26   Sam Houston, 1863 (see page 77)

July 27   Gertrude Stein, 1946

July 28   Johann Sebastian Bach, 1750, and ten in the Empire State Building, 1945 (see page 48)

July 29   Vincent Van Gogh, 1889

July 30   Denis Diderot, 1784 (see page 8)

July 31   Antoine de Saint-Exupéry, 1944

August 1   Theodore Roethke, 1963, and Richard Savage, 1746 (see page 70)

August 2   Warren G. Harding, 1923 (see page 74), Wild Bill Hickok, 1876, and Enrico Caruso, 1921

August 3   Lenny Bruce, 1966

August 4   Hans Christian Andersen, 1875

August 5   Marilyn Monroe, 1962

August 6   Bix Beiderbecke, 1931

August 7   Oliver Hardy, 1957

August 8   Ty Cobb's father, 1904 (shot by Ty Cobb's mother)

August 9   Sharon Tate, 1969

August 10   Estes Kefauver, 1963

August 11   Jackson Pollock, 1956

August 12   William Blake, 1827 (see page 98), and Lord Castlereagh, 1822 (see page 11)

August 13   H. G. Wells, 1946

August 14   Leonard Woolf, 1969 (Virginia's husband)

August 15   Will Rogers, 1935

August 16   Babe Ruth, 1948, and Elvis, 1977

August 17   Conrad Aiken, 1973

August 18   Walter Chrysler, 1940, and Pope Alexander VI, 1503 (see page 117)

August 19   Honoré de Balzac, 1850 (see page 86), Groucho Marx, 1977

August 20   Frank Motto, 1921 (first man to be sentenced to death by a woman judge)

August 21   Leon Trotsky, 1940

Virgo
August 22 to September 22

If you die under the sign of Virgo you will have thought so highly of the purity of your intentions that you considered yourself a superman—others thought you were very nosy. With you it was all or nothing. You either won every fight or lost every case. With such a boom-or-bust life you did a great deal for pancakes, hell, and birth control. All or nothing, you climbed every mountain but couldn't go home again. It's too bad you had only one life to give, and that to marigolds.

August 22	Hot and muggy. Could this have been the night Attila the Hun married a German princess and died in the saddle with her?
August 23	Oscar Hammerstein, 1960
August 24	Pliny the Elder, 79 (see page 37)
August 25	Alfred Kinsey, 1956, and Friedrich Nietzsche, 1900
August 26	Lon Chaney, 1930
August 27	Titian, 1576
August 28	Gracie Allen, 1964
August 29	Brigham Young, 1877 (after twenty-nine wives)
August 30	William Talman (Hamilton Burger), 1968
August 31	Rocky Marciano, 1969
September 1	Martha, the last passenger pigeon, 1914, in the Cincinnati Zoo
September 2	Henri Rousseau, 1910
September 3	e.e. cummings, 1962

September 4   Ho Chi Minh, 1969, and Vince Lombardi, 1970

September 5   Crazy Horse, 1877

September 6   Margaret Sanger, 1966

September 7   Everett Dirksen, 1969

September 8   Charles Henry Packhurst, 1933 (the minister who leapfrogged with whores and died in his ninety-first year after walking off his porch in his sleep)

September 9   Henri de Toulouse-Lautrec, 1901, Mao Zedong, 1976, and William the Conqueror, 1087

September 10   Huey Long, 1935, and Mary Wollstonecraft, 1797 (see page 15)

September 11   Sylvester Graham, 1851 (see page 19)

September 12   Francoise Couperin, 1733

September 13   Michel de Montaigne, 1592 (see page 81)

September 14   Dante, 1321

September 15   Thomas Wolfe, 1938

September 16   John McCormack, 1945 and Maria Callas, 1977

September 17   Charles Pillsbury, 1899

September 18   Peg Entwhistle, 1932 (she leaped off the "D" of the "Hollywood" sign in Los Angeles)

September 19   James A. Garfield, 1881

September 20   Fiorello La Guardia, 1947

September 21   Chief Joseph, 1904

September 22   Nathan Hale, 1776

Libra

September 23 to October 22

If you die under the sign of Libra you will have been pegged a loser. The only way you got ahead was by sleeping no more than four hours at night, putting forks on the left, or it was just one of those things. Without much sex life, you had a love-hate relationship with a white whale. Hard-traveling rebel without a cause, you got under peoples' skins and became a symbol for civilization and its discontents. They named a turnpike plaza after you in New Jersey.

September 23   Sigmund Freud, 1939, Vincenzo Bellini, 1835 (see page 111), and Maria Malibran, 1836 (see page 98)

September 24   Paracelsus, 1541

September 25   Emily Post, 1960

September 26   Daniel Boone, 1820

September 27   Engelbert Humperdinck, 1921

September 28   Herman Melville, 1891

September 29   Emile Zola, 1902 (chimney stopped up, died in his sleep)

September 30   James Dean, 1955

October 1   Marcel Duchamp, 1968

October 2   Freeland Stanley, 1940 (of "Steamer" fame)

October 3   Janis Joplin, 1970 (see page 98)

October 4   Woody Guthrie, 1967

October 5   Robert Dalton, 1892 (of the Dalton Gang — gunned down)

October 6   Alfred, Lord Tennyson, 1892

October 7   Edgar Allan Poe, 1849 (after voting in Baltimore)

October 8   Wendell Willkie, 1944

October 9   Che Guevara, 1967

October 10   Otis Redding, 1967

October 11   Jean Cocteau, and Edith Piaf, both in 1963

October 12   Robert E. Lee, 1870, and Tom Mix, 1940

October 13   Anatole France, 1924

October 14   Judge John Marshall Harlan, 1911 (Superme Court justice who came out of coma, said "Goodbye, I am sorry to have kept you all waiting so long," and died.)

October 15   Cole Porter, 1964

October 16   Marie Antoinette, 1793 (see page 62)

October 17   Frédéric Chopin, 1849

October 18   Thomas Edison, 1931

October 19   Edna St. Vincent Millay, 1950

October 20   Herbert Hoover, 1964, and Eugene V. Debs, 1926

October 21   Jack Kerouac, 1969, and Admiral Horatio Nelson, 1805 (see page 81)

October 22   Paul Cézanne, 1906 (see page 33)

Scorpio

October 23 to November 21

If you die under the sign of Scorpio you will have been the type that liked the little things in life: madeleines, smoke in your eyes, parakeets, canes, the Dodgers, gin, Carole Lombard, and dialectics. You were a man's man or a woman who went far in a man's world, especially if your husband was president or you could shoot. Nothing was elementary to you. So delighted were you with life's variety that you were sure death had no dominion. You were wrong.

October 23	Dutch Schultz, 1935 (see page 19)
October 24	Jackie Robinson, 1972
October 25	Bat Masterson, 1921 (see page 41), and George II, 1760 (see page 81)
October 26	William Hogarth, 1764
October 27	Clifford Holland, 1924 (tunnel builder who died before last tunnel was finished. Guess which tunnel?)
October 28	John Locke, 1704
October 29	Duane Allman, 1971 (king of the bottleneck slide guitar)
October 30	Could this be the day in 54 Claudius ate his fatal ragout?
October 31	Harry Houdini, 1926
November 1	Dale Carnegie, 1955, and Alfred Jarry, 1907 (see page 73)
November 2	Annie Oakley, 1926, and James Thurber, 1961
November 3	Henri Matisse, 1954
November 4	Jerome Kern, 1945 (see page 96)

November 5   Mack Sennett, 1960

November 6   Billy Sunday, 1935

November 7   Eleanor Roosevelt, 1962, and Leo Tolstoy, 1910 (see page 25)

November 8   Nigel Bruce, 1953

November 9   Dylan Thomas, 1953 (see page 8)

November 10   Guillaume Apollinaire, 1918, and Arthur Rimbaud, 1891

November 11   Soren Kierkegaard, 1855

November 12   Elizabeth Gaskell, 1865 (see page 82)

November 13   Gioacchino Rossini, 1868

November 14   Georg Wilhelm Friedrich Hegel, 1831

November 15   Lionel Barrymore, 1954

November 16   Clark Gable, 1960

November 17   Auguste Rodin, 1917

November 18   Marcel Proust, 1922 (see page 12)

November 19   Sylvius, 1672 (he invented gin), and Franz Schubert, 1828 (see page 85)

November 20   Queen Caroline, 1737 (see page 107)

November 21   Robert "Birdman of Alcatraz" Stroud, 1963, and Jakob Böhme, 1624 (see page 115)

Sagittarius
November 22 to December 21

If you die under the sign of Sagittarius you will have lived a life of wild adventure, unless you invented the game of basketball. When your traveling yen was thwarted you resorted to whips, guns, singing mice, huge wheels, or magic flutes. And when that didn't relieve your wanderlust you fathered a country, or lived the life of Riley, or splish-splashed in a bath.

November 22	Jack London, 1916 (suicide), George Ferris, 1896 (a very big wheel), and Aldous Huxley, 1963 (see page 30)
November 23	Governor A.P. Hovey of Indiana, 1891 (he thought he was the reincarnation of Napoleon)
November 24	Hiram Maxim, 1916 (bang bang)
November 25	Diego Rivera, 1957
November 26	John M. Browning, 1926 (bang bang)
November 27	Clement Studebaker, 1901 (putt putt)
November 28	James Naismith, 1939
November 29	Horace Greeley, 1872 (just after losing presidential election)
November 30	Oscar Wilde, 1900
December 1	Alfred T. Mahan, 1914
December 2	Marquis de Sade, 1814
December 3	Robert Louis Stevenson, 1894, and Mary Baker Eddy, 1910 (see page 38)
December 4	George Gipp, 1920 ("The Gipper")

December 5   Wolfgang Amadeus Mozart, 1791 (see page 95), and Vachel Lindsay, 1931 (drank Lysol)

December 6   Anthony Trollope, 1882

December 7   Rube Goldberg, 1970

December 8   Thomas De Quincey, 1859

December 9   Anthony Van Dyck, 1641

December 10   Damon Runyon, 1946

December 11   Oliver Winchester, 1880 (bang bang)

December 12   Tallulah Bankhead, 1968, and Robert Browning, 1889

December 13   Samuel Johnson, 1784

December 14   William Bendix, 1964, and George Washington, 1799 (see page 86)

December 15   Walt Disney, 1966, and Jan Vermeer, 1675

December 16   Sam Cooke, 1964 (see page 57)

December 17   Grigori Rasputin, 1916 (see page 15)

December 18   Louis Moreau Gottschalk, 1869 (see page 111)

December 19   Emily Bronte, 1848 (see page 82)

December 20   Bobby Darin, 1973, and Mayor Richard Daley, 1976

December 21   F. Scott Fitzgerald, 1940, and George Patton, 1945 (bang)

Capricorn

December 22 to January 20

If you die under the sign of Capricorn you will have been a strong person inventing hundreds of tricks for the peanut and billiards cue. This is a very popular sign for presidents to die under. The dead Capricorn woman was probably very innovative. But sex for you, Mr. Lonelyhearts, was seldom more than a wan smile, and in rare cases lady's underwear. Insanity lurked under your strong exterior along with the maltese falcon. Beautiful dreamer, what a lulu of a life.

December 22   Nathanael West, 1940, and Mrs. Andy Jackson, 1828

December 23   Charles Atlas, 1972

December 24   Alban Berg, 1935

December 25   W. C. Fields, 1946

December 26   Harry S Truman, 1972, and Gorgeous George, 1963

December 27   Maurice Ravel, 1937

December 28   Theodore Dreiser, 1945, and Thomas, Lord Macaulay, 1859 (see page 52)

December 29   Jacques David, 1825

December 30   Amelia Jenks Bloomer, 1894

December 31   Giovanni Boccaccio, 1375

January 1   Johann C. Bach, 1782, and Hank Williams, 1953 (see page 101)

January 2   Dick Powell, 1963

January 3   Baldassare Galuppi, 1785 (father of *opera buffa*)

January 4   Albert Camus, 1960, and Calvin Coolidge, 1933

January 5   George Washington Carver, 1963

January 6	Theodore Roosevelt, 1919
January 7	John Berryman, 1972
January 8	Giotto, 1337
January 9	Marco Polo, 1324
January 10	Dashiell Hammett, 1961, and Sinclair Lewis, 1951 (surrounded by nuns in a sanitorium)
January 11	Francis Scott Key, 1843
January 12	Ernie Kovacs, 1962
January 13	James Joyce, 1941, and Stephen Foster, 1864 (see page 96)
January 14	Humphrey Bogart, 1957
January 15	Fannie Farmer, 1915
January 16	Edward Gibbon, 1794 (after draining swollen scrotum)
January 17	Rutherford B. Hayes, 1893, and Chang and Eng, 1874 (Chang died first)
January 18	Rudyard Kipling, 1936, and John Tyler, 1862
January 19	Sidney Greenstreet, 1954
January 20	Robinson Jeffers, 1962

Aquarius
January 21 to February 19

If you die under the sign of Aquarius you will have been a grand schemer and, when things went right, revered as a god. Tax men gave you trouble, along with organized religion, the rest of the National League, and Nelly Bell your jeep. Your revolutionary innovations often became rapidly accepted as part of the very establishment you tried to bring down—but what better place to go back-to-school shopping than your store?

January 21	C.B. De Mille, 1959 (while making a film about the Boy Scouts)
January 22	LBJ, 1973
January 23	William Pitt, 1806 (see page 29), and David Graham Phillips, 1911 (see page 51)
January 24	Winston Churchill, 1965
January 25	Al Capone, 1947
January 26	William Wrigley, 1932
January 27	Giuseppe Verdi, 1901
January 28	Charlemagne, 814
January 29	H.L. Mencken, 1956, and Henry Murger, 1861 (see page 104)
January 30	Betsy Ross, 1836, and Charles I, 1649 (see page 59)
January 31	Samuel Goldwyn, 1974
February 1	Hedda Hopper, 1966
February 2	Bertrand Russell, 1970
February 3	Woodrow Wilson, 1924, and Buddy Holly and the Big Bopper, 1959 (see page 56)

February 4   Thomas Carlyle, 1889

February 5   Paul Hardmuth, 1962 (see *Dr. Blood's Coffin*)

February 6   Gustav Klimt, 1918

February 7   Harvey Firestone, 1938

February 8   Gee Jon, 1924 (first man to die in a gas chamber)

February 9   Fyodor Dostoevsky, 1881, and Gabby Hayes, 1969

February 10   Aleksandr Pushkin, 1837

February 11   René Descartes, 1650

February 12   J. C. Penney, 1971, Immanuel Kant, 1804 (see page 83), and Lady Jane Grey, 1554

February 13   Richard Wagner, 1883

February 14   Captain James Cook, 1779 (see page 26)

February 15   Petroleum Vesuvius Nasby, 1888 (the Woody Allen of the Gilded Age)

February 16   Eddie Foy, 1928 (while playing in *A Fallen Star*)

February 17   Geronimo, 1909, and Heinrich Heine, 1856 (see page 69)

February 18   Martin Luther, 1546, and Andy Devine, 1977

February 19   André Gide, 1951

Pisces

February 20 to March 20

If you die under the sign of Pisces you will have had great facility of expression, unless you stayed in the British Museum too long. You carried an unwarranted reputation for sex mania; was it your fault Dagwood married a knockout blonde, and that Raymond Burr wasn't the apple of ladies' eyes? Misunderstood though you were, many monuments remain in your memory (and a lot have been torn down). All in all, you were easy to get down if properly strained.

February 20   Walter Winchell, 1972

February 21   Nikolai Gogol, 1852 (see page 77)

February 22   Charles Wilson Peale, 1827 (after twenty-two portraits of George Washington)

February 23   Stan Laurel, 1965

February 24   Robert Fulton, 1815

February 25   Christopher Wren, 1723

February 26   Fernandel, 1971

February 27   Aleksandr Borodin, 1887 (A stranger in Paradise?)

February 28   Henry Luce, 1967, and Henry James, 1916

February 29   Frank Albertson, 1964 (see *Junior G-Men of the Air*)

March 1   Gabriele D'Annunzio, 1938 (died bored)

March 2   D.H. Lawrence, 1930 (see page 26), and John Wesley, 1791 (see page 104)

March 3   Leonard Warren, 1960 (see page 34)

March 4   William Carlos Williams, 1963

March 5   Josef Stalin, 1953, Thomas Arne, 1778 (see page 103), and the Mad Poet of Broadway, 1842 (see page 19)

March 6   Louisa May Alcott, 1888 (see page 65)

"Della, call Paul Drake and tell him to meet me at the Crescent City Motel."
"Yes, chief." The secretary dialed. "Paul Drake, please."
 Mason was almost out the door.
"Perry!" Della stopped him. "Paul Drake is dead."
 RIP William Hopper, 1971 (of a heart attack)

March 7   Railroad Bill, 1907 (see page 11)

March 8   Hector Berlioz, 1869

March 9   Saint Thomas Aquinas' donkey, 1274 (see page 25)

March 10   Bull Connor, 1973, and Harriet Tubman, 1913

March 11   Erle Stanley Gardner, 1970

March 12   Cesare Borgia, 1507 (see page 62), and Charlie "Bird" Parker, 1955 (some say he was watching TV in the Baroness Pannonica de Koenigswarter's apartment, some say he was doing something else; either way, Bird to Paradise)

March 13   Clarence Darrow, 1938

March 14   Karl Marx, 1883 ("Last words are for fools who haven't said enough")

March 15   Chic Young, 1973, and Lincoln Beachey, 1915 (see page 47)

March 16   Daniel Gerber, 1974

March 17   Ivan the Terrible, 1584 (see page 47)

March 18   King Farouk, 1965 (see page 7)

March 19   Edgar Rice Burroughs, 1950

March 20   Chet Huntley, 1974

Good Night